The Effective
Use of
ROLE-PLAY

The Effective Use of ROLE-PLAY

Practical Techniques for Improving Learning

Second edition

Morry van Ments

KOGAN
PAGE

To Jennifer, Mark, Keren and Elizabeth

'He who knows he has enough is rich'
Lao Tsu Tao Te Ching

YOURS TO HAVE AND TO HOLD

BUT NOT TO COPY

First published in Great Britain in 1983 and reprinted in 1984 and 1987
Revised edition published in 1989, reprinted in 1990 and published in paperback in 1994
Second edition published in 1999

Kogan Page Limited
120 Pentonville Road
London N1 9JN

© Morry van Ments, 1999

British Library Cataloguing in Publication Data

A CIP record for this book is available from the British Library.

ISBN 0 7494 2799 X

Typeset by Kogan Page
Printed and bound by Biddles Ltd, Guildford and King's Lynn

Contents

Contents

Foreword

One of the most fruitful ways of generating new matter is by a cross-fertilization of subject areas. This book came from a realization that role-play was being used in a variety of ways by people who rarely came across each other to exchange experiences. It was clear that although industrial trainers, school teachers, college lecturers and youth leaders were dealing with very different students and for very different reasons, their techniques had a great deal in common and they could each benefit from a distillation of the best practices in all fields.

The other objective of this book is to set forth the full range of role-play methods available, together with an indication of the advantages and limitations inherent in them. All too often one sticks closely to the well-worn tracks that have proved so comforting in the past without realizing that there are other and sometimes better ways, which may be more suited to the particular teaching task in hand.

Teaching is an integrated experience and the intended end of a lesson governs the way it begins as much as the beginning governs the end. Except in the highly controlled environment of programmed learning every part of a session relates backwards and forwards to the other parts. It is therefore artificial to pretend that the course of running a role-play is entirely a linear process. For convenience in writing, however, this book follows a logic which is desirable if not always attainable. After a discussion in Chapters 1 and 2 of the concept of role and an outline of role-play as a technique to be used within the larger framework of teaching, Chapter 3 argues the need for a systematic approach. The following chapter stresses the importance of identifying the type of role-play which is being used so that appropriate methods may be used with it. Chapters 5 to 8 form the core of practical advice: they go through the process of writing, running and debriefing a role-play. The remaining chapters deal with particular aspects of role-play and the way in which it is used.

Those who want to get quickly into the practicalities of running role-plays should therefore first read Chapter 3 and then go straight on to Chapters 5 to 8. Otherwise the book is designed to be read in a normal sequence, with tables at key intervals in the text and brief examples that will form quick reference points in the future. There are a number of other books (Ladousse, 1987; Aston 1985, Maier, 1975; Milroy, 1982; Towers, 1969; Shafter 1976) which have lengthy and detailed accounts of sample role-plays and no attempt has been made to duplicate the work of these authors.

A problem that presented itself was what to call the person in charge of the role-play. The terms teacher, trainer, leader, facilitator, lecturer, organizer are all commonly used to describe such a person. Unfortunately, the use of each of these terms carries with it implications about the attitudes of the person so described, together with presumptions about the type of student they are dealing with. Since the intention behind the book is to stress the universality of role-play methods the more neutral terms 'tutor' and 'student' are used throughout.

Finally it was decided that the most important thing was clarity and ease of communication. To that end it was felt that language is a symbolic convention and to follow the conventions to which the reader is accustomed provides for the greatest ease in reading. Nevertheless, the decision to use the male pronoun throughout does not invalidate in any way the argument in Chapter 6 for care in the allocation and writing of roles.

The author of a book of this sort is bound to be indebted to the many people who have helped to make it possible. I would like to acknowledge my debt to Ed Berman who first filled me with enthusiasm for the use of games and simulations as teaching techniques, to those who showed me their methods at conferences of the Society for the Advancement of Gaming and Simulation in Education and Training (SAGSET), and to Donna Brandes who helped me to an increased awareness of, and sensitivity to, group needs.

During the writing of the book I was able to talk to a number of people who used role-play in their teaching and work; their encouragement and advice were always stimulating. In particular I would like to thank Joan Sullivan (National Marriage Guidance Council), Michael Morrish (Haberdashers' Aske's School), Christine Casey (Eckington School), Donald McLeod (Civil Service Commission) and Amanda Stafford (Mapperley Hospital).

My path has been made easier by the support and friendship of

David Walker and Jetta Megarry, both of SAGSET, and above all by the wholehearted backing which I have had from my colleagues at the Centre for Extension Studies, Loughborough University, who have carried extra work loads themselves in order to enable me to finish this book.

Finally I would like to thank my secretary, Lynne Atkinson, whose cheerfulness and efficiency have made the writing of this book more of a delight than a chore, and my family who kept me relatively sane even when I must have been driving them mad.

Preface to the second edition

In the period since the first edition of this book it has become the standard text for those wishing to develop or improve their skills in using role-play. This new edition has therefore retained the core content of the original, but incorporates a number of improvements and changes designed to give it a more practical character.

The original Chapters 9 and 10 have been condensed and amalgamated into one chapter, which surveys uses of role-play outside conventional education and training. Chapter 11 on linked role-play has become increasingly irrelevant to today's practical needs and has been dropped. These changes have left space for a new Chapter 10, which looks at the potential for using computers and the Internet as tools to widen the scope of role-play.

A number of Hints, Tips and Warnings have been introduced to help the reader. In some cases these give additional practical advice, in others they highlight key points made in the text.

Changes continue to be made in each revision to ensure that the book is non-sexist. A better balance has also been struck between role-play used for education and for training. The major part of the book, however, remains of equal value to primary school teachers, university lecturers, and industrial trainers.

There is still a crucial need for more and better training in the use of role-play and I hope that this book will continue to help satisfy that need.

Morry van Ments, 1999

1 *Roles and role-playing*

Introduction

Compared with the number of books on other subjects there is a relative dearth of literature on specific techniques of teaching. Perhaps this is because the idea of teaching, of passing on knowledge, attitudes, skills and behavioural routines, seems to be such a natural one. We all enjoy showing someone else how to do something. Everyone has answered another person's question or demonstrated an idea or technique. Therefore everyone, in a sense, is a teacher.

The transmission of knowledge is part of the everyday business of living; it has probably changed little over the centuries indicating that informal teaching has been going on since the dawn of civilization. Systems of formal education and training, however, have not only expanded to cover more people, (in particular there has been a dramatic rise in the participation rate in UK universities), but over the years education has become increasingly expensive. Not unnaturally, there has been a corresponding demand for heightened efficiency in the process of transmitting knowledge, skills and attitudes.

For many years education was synonymous with textbooks, lectures, blackboard and chalk. Similarly training was identified with practical demonstration, practice, lists of procedures and workshop manuals. Trainers knew how the thing should be done; trainers knew the answers. Since they knew the logic behind the process or system that was being learnt it seemed reasonable to suppose that the same logical order should be used in teaching the subject. Whilst the job of the trainer was to present a set of facts, methods, ideas in a given 'best' logical order, the job of the student was to become proficient by a process of repetition and memorizing.

But a number of factors have combined to change the face of education and training and open the way to new ideas and techniques. There have been developments in the technical equipment used to present knowledge to the student: films, television, computers, audio-cassettes, teletext, microfiche, videodisc, CD-Roms, and the Internet. Many of these have encouraged an expanding interest in the idea of open learning and corresponding changes within the education system.

Parallel with this, the role of the teacher has been closely questioned and answers sought to the following types of question.

- Should each teaching session be tightly structured?
- Should learning be teacher-centred, or student-centred?
- How much of learning is concerned with facts; how much with attitudes; how much with application of skills?
- How can learning be made active rather than passive?
- How can classroom learning be related to real life?
- Can self-motivation be built into learning?

Another aspect of teaching which has been in a state of flux is the concept of group learning as against individual learning. In many fields it has been accepted that the dynamics of a team or group enable its members to learn from one another. Working as part of a group can heighten the individual's understanding of the subject and facilitate the transition from theoretical background to practical application.

Out of all these cross-currents has grown a feeling that there is a place in many, if not all, areas of education for techniques that focus on the student and his understanding, that involve him in activity within a group, that relate learning to practice and practice to real life. In the UK the development of GNVQs (General National Vocational Qualifications) has led to course work in many areas being more project based and work related. Another new development which emphasises experience, has been APEL (the Accreditation of Prior Experiential Learning). These initiatives have a common element stressing a move away from didactic forms of instruction and towards techniques which provide practical experience. Simulations and games go some way towards providing these techniques. They are one way of pursuing the tenet 'I hear and I forget; I see and I remember; I do and I understand'.

Simulation and gaming

The use of role-play as an educational or training technique is part of the wider set of techniques that have collectively become known as simulation and gaming. These are techniques which aim to provide the student with either a highly simplified reproduction of part of a real or imaginary world (a simulation) or a structured system of competitive play that incorporates the material to be learnt (a game).

Their use is nothing new. The idea of using a game to reflect the problems of the real world goes back at least as far as 3000 BC to the Chinese game of Wei-Hai -now known by the Japanese name of Go – and other more recent games such as Chess which represent the beginnings of war-gaming. War-gaming became very sophisticated in the form of the nineteenth century Kriegspiel which had hundreds of rules and thousands of pieces and was used to train the Prussian military. Nowadays such war-games use computers and are played on a vast scale. Similarly, business gaming developed in the early 1960s and has become widespread as a method of teaching a range of subjects in management schools.

More recently the use of simulations and games has spread to school and youth work. Originally in America, and now to an increasing extent in Britain, they are being used in the teaching of geography, history, chemistry, mathematics, social studies, religious studies, politics, Third World studies, indeed almost any subject. They may be found in primary schools and in universities, in youth clubs and in trade union classes. These games and simulations use a wide variety of formats. They may resemble card games such as Snap or Rummy; they may have the same framework as Bingo or Dominoes, or use a board as in Monopoly or Snakes and Ladders. The simulations may use cardboard models, chance events generated by dice or computer, messages sent by telephone, letters or memos, or a large cast of players to represent the inhabitants of a town and the officials with whom they come into contact.

Many simulations involve students in making decisions and communicating or negotiating with one another. These students provide the human element in the system that is being studied and they are expected to react to the situation in a way that will be determined by how they and the other participants see their relative position, motivations and attitudes – in other words how they see their role within the system. Role-play is the name given to one particular type of simulation that focuses attention on the interaction of people with one another. It emphasizes the functions performed by different people under various circumstances.

Some innovations in education and training such as the use of closed circuit television, programmed learning and, more recently, computers, were greeted on their arrival by a mass of publicity both in the educational press and by the general media. Not only that but this attention and publicity has continued for a considerable time.

Every week there appear news items and comment on developments in these and allied fields. The most recent of these innovations is the CD-ROM. Yet a similar revolution has been taking place in the use of simulation and gaming as teaching techniques; in particular there has been a quiet burgeoning in the use of role-play as a flexible, cheap and easy device for instruction.

The advances in the use of role-play which have taken place in numerous areas such as schools, colleges, industrial training, youth clubs, health and social education, have largely been unheralded and given little publicity. One suspects that expense and complication attract attention rather more than simplicity. Whatever the reason, the lack of comment and criticism has led to two shortcomings which have differing origins. In the first place there are many who are poised on the brink of using role-play in their teaching but would like the reassurance of a guide to show them the way and help distinguish between short cuts and blind alleys. In the second place there are those who are already well along the road but who would like to know how role-play can be used in other contexts, more efficiently, and without some of the problems that can occur when exercises are used without a clear understanding of their characteristics.

The intention in the following chapters is to provide some guidelines and advice for both of these groups, and thus enable teachers and trainers to use role-play in an effective way and achieve their objectives with the minimum of stress and the maximum of enjoyment.

Role-play

The idea of role-play, in its simplest form, is that of asking someone to imagine that they are either themselves or another person in a particular situation. They are then asked to behave exactly as they feel that person would. As a result of doing this they, or the rest of the class, or both, will learn something about the person and/or situation. In essence, each player acts as part of the social environment of the others and provides a framework in which they can test out their repertoire of behaviours or study the interacting behaviour of the group.

From this deceptively simple concept spring a large number of alternative approaches. To begin with, role-players may take on the roles of imaginary people, real people, or themselves. They may find themselves playing opposite one or more people who may similarly be taking a wide range of parts, including possibly playing themselves or even the role-player.

Situations may be simple or elaborate, familiar or strange. They may be described in detail or left to the imagination of the role-player. The action may be played out fully and last for days; it may be a fragment and last for minutes. The learning which takes place may be first-hand or second-hand; it may be acquired by participation or observation. What is learnt may be a skill or technique, or it may be more in the nature of sensitization or change of attitude. At the end of a role-play, therefore, it may only be necessary to ensure that the session is brought to a reasonable close; on the other hand the tutor may have to spend a lot of time helping the group to appreciate the implications of what has happened, or it may be appropriate to re-run the role-play in order to practise some modified behaviour.

Role-player	Imaginary person	
	Real person	(a) outside learning group
		(b) within learning group
	Self	
Situation	Simple, one-to-one/Complex	
	Familiar/New	
	Detailed/Outline	
	Short/Long	
Learning	First-hand (participative)/Vicarious (observed)	
	Skill, technique	
	Sensitization	
	Attitude change	

Figure 1.1 Dimensions of role-play

The alternatives in these three dimensions – role, situation and learning function – are listed in Figure 1. 1. The differences between the types lead to differences of approach in setting-up, running and discussing the role-play, and these will be explored in more detail later in the book.

First, however, we must take a closer look at the concept of role, the way it acts as a framework for social interaction, and the way in which we learn to use it from earliest childhood. It is only a short step from there to the use of role-play as a teaching technique.

Concept of role

The origin of the word 'role' derives from the word used to describe the roll of parchment on which an actor's part was written. It therefore descends directly from theatrical use meaning an actor's part in a drama. When watching a play the audience needs to be able to identify quickly the heroes and the villains; they want to know the position of each character – whether king, farmer, mother, great-aunt or grandson. These titles or roles are often indicated on the cast list before the play even begins. The extension of the concept of role to the way people behave in everyday life comes from a similar need in real life for people to summarize or condense what may be complex perceptions of the constituent details of another person's appearance or behaviour.

Throughout our waking lives we are exposed to a bombardment of sensations far greater in quantity than we can cope with. The brain has mechanisms for coding and grouping this information so that we can make comparisons and decisions. This process is called perception. We attach symbols and names to these simplified packets of information so that, for example, we may see a pink coloured shape of a certain size moving gently in a current of air; what we perceive is a rose. The concept of role acts as a shorthand way of identifying and labelling a set of appearances and behaviours on the assumption that these appearances and behaviours are characteristic of a particular person and predictable within a given situation.

In everyday life roles may be ascribed to people in a variety of ways. They may for example be allocated by social position such as teacher, husband, storeman, cleaner, priest, infant, juvenile delinquent. Often these roles imply reciprocal relationships: husband and wife, mother and child, doctor and patient, delinquent and police officer. A role is then a way of expressing group norms and the social pressures acting on an individual or group. It characterizes a person's social behaviour.

Sometimes role is defined in terms of the context in which people find themselves such as a church, concert hall, football match, holiday camp, school or office so that people see themselves as members of a congregation, an audience, football supporters, holiday-makers, students or office workers. The role behaviour of an individual changes in accordance with his surroundings – the role behaviour of a congregation is different to that of a football crowd.

Role may also be defined in terms of function or purpose. The people who are to be found in a hospital may be carrying out the tasks of doctor, administrator, patient, visitor or chaplain.

Role-taking

When people take a particular role they are using a repertoire of behaviours which are expected of that role. A doctor asks questions, performs physical examinations, gives advice, prescribes medicines, carries out emergency treatment; a police officer arrests people, gives advice, directs traffic, wears a uniform. This behaviour is often the result of internalizing the expectations developed by others – in other words doing what other people expect of the person in that role. It is a major strategy for understanding, and thus predicting, the behaviour of others, and when other people act 'out of role', as when a manager cries, or a priest uses swear words, they upset our expectations. Moreover, one of the commonest causes of interpersonal conflict is the misinterpretation of another's behaviour. It is therefore important for people to identify the framework of such behaviour and hence whether it is in accordance with the role which one assumes the other person is taking.

The process of role-taking is a natural and continuous one for anyone who is socialized within their community. It is a serious matter; most of our social life consists of such activity and failure to adapt to the right role at the right time can lead to a breakdown in communication. A conversation, for example, depends on each person anticipating the other's feelings, expectancies, thoughts and probable reaction to their own behaviour. This enables each to guide and monitor the conversation, otherwise the participants would only be talking at each other as small children do. The ability to predict the other person's response is partly aided by an awareness of the role they are taking at that particular time.

Of course a person's role will change throughout their life and indeed throughout the day. The wife says good morning to her husband; the children have breakfast with their father; the postman delivers to an addressee; the police officer directs the motorist; the shopkeeper greets a customer; the commissionaire salutes a manager and the secretary says hello to her boss. The husband, father, addressee, motorist, customer, manager and boss are all the same person who in the evening may be first violinist, scout, college student or a hundred and one other things. Similarly a person may be wife, daughter, driver, judge, golfer and television viewer all in the course of the same day. Their behaviour at any given moment will indicate to others which role they are playing, and they in turn will adjust that behaviour to comply with what they feel others expect.

> **TIP** Introduce the idea of role-play by discussing the range of roles participants take in real life.

Just because roles in everyday life are largely determined by a person's surrounding culture and his position in it does not mean that his role behaviour will always truly correspond to his disposition and feelings. It is a common observation that people dissimulate and pretend to be a different sort of person to what they really are. The head teacher may have to put on an appearance of severity even though within himself he is highly amused at the pupil's latest escapade. Role-taking may therefore infer both a natural inclination towards a set of behaviours and a deliberate following of guidelines in order to create a given impression. In that sense the role-taker may at times 'act out' being a president, judge, shopkeeper or doctor.

Role-playing

The idea of role-playing derives from this everyday activity. In role-playing one is practising a set of behaviours which is considered appropriate to a particular role. It is a natural part of children's behaviour and everyone will have experienced it as part of their childhood games. As Ladousse (1987) puts it: the idea of 'role' is that of taking part in a specific situation, the idea of 'play' is associated with a safe environment and encouraging creativity.

There is an unfortunate confusion between role-playing and acting. The essential difference is that acting consists of bringing to life a dramatist's ideas (or one's own ideas) in order to influence and entertain an audience, whereas role-play is the experiencing of a problem under an unfamiliar set of constraints in order that one's own ideas may emerge and one's understanding increase.

Actors train their voice and body so that, like the athlete or singer, they are completely under their own control. They then use their talents as instruments to interpret a message or an emotion. Whatever actors do, the effect it will have on the audience is at the forefront of their mind. Will it make the audience laugh or cry? Will it deceive them into thinking the butler committed the murder? Will they become more sympathetic or antagonistic to this character? In the course of exploring a script the actor needs to consider the interaction of characters, their background and motivation. But at the end of the period of study and rehearsal the objective is always the same: to move and influence the audience, to entertain and divert them.

The purpose of the role-player is very different. Role-players are not concerned with an audience, only with themselves and other role-players. Their aim is to feel, react and behave as closely as possible to the way someone placed in that particular situation would do. They are only concerned with the effects of their behaviour on the other players, not an audience, and will do whatever is necessary within their role to persuade and convince them that their ideas and decisions are important. As long as they give their fellow role-players sufficient information and an indication of their attitudes and wishes, they do not have to convince them that they have been miraculously transformed into another person. Thus the 'acting out' in role-playing is, for all practical purposes, no greater than that which is done by the majority of people from time to time in the course of their everyday lives.

The idea of role-playing is very simple: to give students the opportunity to practise interacting with others in certain roles. The situation is defined by producing a scenario and a set of role-descriptions. The scenario gives a background to the particular problem or environment and indicates the constraints which operate. The role-descriptions give profiles of the people involved.

The role-play can be run for a few minutes, up to half an hour or even longer. At the end there is a debriefing session in which observers may comment on the way in which the characters behaved and the lessons to be drawn from this. The players themselves will always take an important part in this debriefing.

As a technique, role-play has proved to be very powerful. It is highly motivating and enables students to put themselves in situations they have never experienced before; in particular it opens the way for them to put themselves in others' shoes. Much of our behaviour in interpersonal interactions is governed by our assumptions about our own role, other people's roles, and the way we perceive these roles. It is natural therefore that when we want to teach subjects which involve interpersonal behaviour we should turn to role-playing as a potent teaching technique. It can be used at different levels to teach simple skills of communication to show how people interact and their stereotyping of others, and to explore deep personal blocks and emotions.

Because the technique is so powerful, it is essential that tutors and trainers approach it in a systematic way and are aware of the different ways of using it. As with any other tool there are better and worse ways of using it. It is important to use the right type of role-play to fit the specific circumstances or training objectives. Some types of role-play are best suited to skills training, others to increasing sensitivity towards individuals and groups, and some to enabling students to explore their own attitudes and emotions. Clearly it can be ineffective and even dangerous to use the wrong technique for a particular group and in particular to avoid drifting into some of the more specialized uses discussed in Chapter 9.

Before using role-play as a technique to aid learning, we should be clear in our minds that we are not dealing with the therapeutic aspects as used by the psychotherapist, nor with prepared or improvised drama, nor problem solving case studies. We are looking at the simple use of role-play to enable the student to experiment with interaction as it occurs in the real world.

The next chapter shows how role-play fits into the rest of the learning experience, its strengths and weaknesses, and how tutors and trainers need to develop their own skills for this specialized form of teaching.

2 The place of role-play in teaching and training

Why use role-play?

The most important question to be asked when considering the use of a particular teaching technique is why you want, or perhaps do not want, to use that particular technique. The key issue is how it fits into the whole learning process. The teacher will organize that process into a curriculum, the trainer into a course or training programme, the youth leader or social worker into a programme of activities. Whatever it is called, it will consist of a number of activities and resources planned to be used in a certain sequence in order to achieve a series of objectives, and it is these objectives that must determine the appropriate teaching methods to be used.

Although conventional methods of teaching and learning such as lectures, reading, films, discussions and writing can be used successfully to help students acquire knowledge of factual material and the essential theoretical framework into which future experiences may be fitted, they are incomplete in at least two major respects.

In the first place they cannot easily help to change the student's attitude or behaviour. To read or hear about something is not the same as experiencing it, and it is often only by actual experience that understanding and change can come about. It is easy, for example, to have an intellectual grasp of deprivation and poverty, or to discuss the feelings of those who are disadvantaged or oppressed. To actually experience being powerless or discriminated against is a different matter. Students may criticize those who are destitute for not acting, not using their initiative; when they have experienced the frustration of being in a similar situation themselves they will have more sympathy and understanding towards it. The concept of impotence is vastly different from the reality.

Another example might be from the training of managers. The trainee manager may respond to a question or case study by saying how he or she would handle a disgruntled employee; it is a very salutary experience to have to actually do so. Role-play is one of a unique group of experiential teaching techniques which help the student to cope with handling human situations and uncertainty.

Role-play places the student in a situation, which imposes the same type of constraints, motivations and pressures that exist in the real world; it can be used in a variety of teaching situations. Historical material, literature, sociology, economics, politics, management, geography, may all be illuminated by means of simulated activities which involve the student in a framework of events designed to emphasize the environment in which people find themselves, thus throwing light on their behaviour.

The second major area where conventional methods need to be supplemented is that of transferable interpersonal and communication skills. No matter how much reading and observing the student undertakes, the only way to develop these skills fully is by using them in actual inter-personal situations. The interplay of verbal and non-verbal behaviour is far too complex and subtle to be reduced to a few simple rules, and even if such a thing were easy it would still not be possible for students to improve without receiving continuous feedback on their behaviour. The interpretation of, and reaction to, the signals received back from other people contain the keys to effective inter-personal communication.

There are many types of situation where practical experience is used by tutors to help students develop their interpersonal skills. There are individual situations such as counselling, interviews, customer service and sales, personal relationships; there are also group situations such as committees, negotiations, public meetings, team working or group interviews. The range of students who can benefit is limitless, from those with learning difficulties to doctors, managers, police and research workers. Few would deny that interpersonal skills are amongst the most valuable assets for any person to have.

Role-play is ideally suited to provide the necessary experience. Its virtues have been listed by several authors but perhaps the most comprehensive list is that provided by Chesler and Fox (1966) from which the following comments have been derived.

Advantages of role-play

A summary of the advantages of role-play is given in Figure 2.1. Although the list appears to give a set of discrete items, these may be grouped under three main headings.

---

1. Enables student to express hidden feelings.
2. Enables student to discuss private issues and problems.
3. Enables student to empathize with others and understand their motivations.
4. Gives practice in various types of behaviour.
5. Portrays generalized social problems and dynamics of group interaction, formal and informal.
6. Gives life and immediacy to academic descriptive material (history, English, economics, geography).
7. Provides opportunity for non-articulate students and emphasizes importance of non-verbal, emotional responses.
8. Motivational and effective because it involves activity.
9. Provides rapid feedback for both student and tutor.
10. Is student-centred and addresses itself to the needs and concerns of the trainee; the group can control content and pace.
11. Closes gap between training and real life situations.
12. Changes attitudes.
13. Permits training in the control of feelings and emotions.

Figure 2.1 Advantages of role-play

Positive and safe in dealing with attitudes and feelings

In the first place role-play exposes attitudes and feelings in a way which is both positive and safe: positive because they are acknowledged as a legitimate area for discussion and analysis and also because the role-play itself provides an opportunity to learn how to control those feelings and emotions; safe because the student's own behaviour is not at issue – it is the behaviour of the student-in-role which is being discussed. However narrow a margin there is between the two, it is always within the power of tutors, by the way they conduct the session, to ensure that students are protected against appearing foolish, or being censured for their attitudes.

Suppose the role-play scenario concerns the choice of someone who is black, Jewish or female to become a section leader. The selectors may be managers, personnel officers or a selection committee. No doubt in the course of the interview and selection discussions a number of things will be said about the suitability of the candidate. Some of these things will be free of prejudice, others will display distinct signs of bias. It is a common experience in this type of role-play that the participants will be able to identify some of their prejudices some of the time, but at other times they will not recognize what they are doing as being biased. In the debriefing of the exercise observers will be able to ask 'Why did you question her about her husband's job – would you have asked a man about his wife's job?', or 'Did you realize you were just satisfying your own curiosity when you asked about arrangements for lunch?', or 'Why did you make a point of asking the black candidate questions about possible contacts with the police?'.

If the debriefing is properly conducted, the role-players will be able to answer these questions in relation to the role they played. Indeed, if the tutor feels that the group is treading on sensitive ground, they can be steered towards phrasing the questions in a slightly different way, eg 'Why did the manager (or you as manager) question her about her husband's job?'. Thus, although it is clear that questions about prejudice have been raised for the individual player, he can keep the more painful ones to himself and shelter behind his role during the public discussion. The role-play opens up the issue both as a private concern and a public debate but enables the two domains to be kept separate if the tutor so desires.

Relates closely to the outside world

Another major advantage of role-play over more conventional methods is its ability to relate closely to the outside world. Because it reflects behavioural patterns which the student may actually need to use when she has finished training, or which she may need to deal with in others, it enables her to gain practical experience and rehearse skills she will require in the future. Not only is it possible to try out one's skill in dealing with a customer, negotiating with a union representative, being interviewed for a job or chairing a meeting, it is also possible to repeat the experience and hence improve one's performance. The use of role-play brings home to the student that some aspects of behaviour, such as the development of good human relations, require specific skills in the same sense that operating a machine or playing golf requires skill. Moreover it demonstrates that these skills can be taught – they are not something that people are born with. The emphasis in role-play is on requiring students to do and to act, rather than just talk about something.

Highly motivating

The major advantage of role-play is the one it shares with all simulation and gaming activities in that it is highly motivating and gives students simple, direct and rapid feedback on the effects of their actions. Provided that the role-play is well organized and operated the participants invariably enjoy it, become involved in it and remember it long after they have forgotten much of the learning which they obtained in other ways. The motivational aspect of role-play and simulation is the central aspect which all teachers, trainers and other users comment upon. And if you motivate the student to learn then half the battle is won.

TIP Ask students after a year or two which parts of the training programme they remember and which parts taught them things of which they have since made use. Use the responses to adjust the balance of your training programme.

Disadvantages of role-play

Figure 2.2 gives a summary of the potential disadvantages of role-play. These centre around three areas of concern. The one which is usually in the forefront of people's minds is the effect that using role-play may have on the atmosphere and conventions of the classroom. This is the issue of whether teaching should be seen as 'serious', and the question of social and authority relationships between teacher and taught. The fact that most students enjoy role-plays may be seen by some as a threat to the staid and earnest atmosphere of the class-room. Likewise, if the role-play portrays a historical event in which some of the participants revolt, or if the scene is a confrontation between bosses and unions, then students are likely to get caught up in the emotion of the moment and the normal relationships between teacher and taught may change with a consequential breakdown in the normal discipline of the classroom.

HINT Chapter 7 looks at ways of dealing with classroom problems

1. Tutor loses control over what is learnt and the order in which it is learnt.
2. Simplifications can mislead.
3. Uses a large amount of time.
4. Uses other resources – people, space, special items
5. Depends on the quality of tutor and student.
6. Impact may trigger off withdrawal or defence symptoms.
7. May be seen as too entertaining or frivolous.
8. May dominate learning to the exclusion of solid theory and facts.
9. May depend on what students already know.

Figure 2.2 Disadvantages of role-play

A second issue concerns the accuracy and relevance of what is learnt and the degree to which the teacher or trainer must be in control of what is being learnt. Take a specific example: the scenario is a public meeting in which the issue of environmental pollution by a local industrial plant is to be discussed. The meeting has been called by a government inspector who is holding an inquiry into a planning application for expansion of the plant.

This scenario could be used:

● with school children to introduce them to the idea of pollution as a matter for public concern;
● with college students to teach them the formal procedures followed in a public inquiry;
● with environmental health or factory inspectors as a focal point for studying methods of measuring pollution;

- with company secretaries or legal advisors to explore ways of working within the law whilst expanding their businesses;
- with community rights workers to give them advocacy skills with which to argue their case.

All of these are distinct learning experiences which happen to use the same scenario. If all goes well then everyone will be happy. But suppose that in the course of the simulation the government representatives do a deal with the representatives of the factory? Do the school children learn about compromise and the reality of industrial life at an age when they cannot cope with the knowledge? Or what happens when the community rights workers in their role-play get bogged down in a morass of technical detail on measuring pollution? Or should the company legal experts spend a lot of their time debating the morality, as distinct from the legality, of anti-pollution measures?

! WARNING !

Always ensure that there is an opportunity to clear up factual errors that role-players may make. This may be done in the debriefing, or by producing a fact sheet for reference during or after the role-play.

It is possible of course to put constraints on the role-play so that participants cannot stray too far from the intended path. The greater the constraints, however, the less effective the role-play is likely to be. It is the power of the imagination which enhances the effects of role-play situations.

The third main area of disadvantage is that of resources. Role-play tends to use large amounts of time, space and sometimes people. In the first place, the process of warming-up and getting students accustomed to the idea of role-play cannot be rushed. This is particularly true of those who are meeting it for the first time, but even the experienced user will generally do some preliminary exercises before going into the main role-play. In the second place the process itself needs time to develop and in the third place it is essential to allow sufficient time for discussion after the event. So ample time must be allowed if the tutor wants to use role-play as part of the teaching strategy.

> **TIP** In the industrial training context where 'time is money', it is useful to point to the cost of mistakes made by poorly trained employees and the benefits of having already experienced a problem situation.

Room requirements will vary. The essential requirement is a flat-floored room. A tiered lecture room is inhibiting to say the least and constrains the type of exercise which can be used. The requirement for a flat-floored room is usually not too difficult to meet but there are sometimes other needs which relate to the size of the room or the availability of a suite of rooms which can be used in conjunction with one another.

Many role-play exercises can be run successfully by a single tutor. The role of observers can be delegated to students as can the other subsidiary roles within the role-play. Sometimes, however, the complexity of the role-play or special circumstances which demand specialist knowledge, require the involvement of other members of staff or outside help. In these cases the demands of role-play will inevitably be greater than those of more conventional methods of teaching.

> **TIP** Helpers need not always be drawn from among your colleagues. 'Real' people from outside – sportsmen, shopkeepers, managers, office workers etc can be asked to volunteer their assistance. It is fun for them and brings in another viewpoint.

Finally there are more constraints on numbers of students than in conventional teaching or lecturing. It becomes increasingly unsatisfactory as a technique once numbers rise above 20 to 25 students, although there are always exceptions.

Subject areas

Let us assume that the tutor has studied the advantages and disadvantages of using role-play and has decided that there might be a possible application within their subject areas. What are the most likely subjects and situations in which this technique could be used?

As with any teaching technique, this is largely a matter of personal preference and choice. The following notes will help to point tutors who are new to role-play in the right direction, and indicate to them which are the most likely areas in which to succeed. They should not be taken as a list of what can and cannot be done with role-play. Given enough imagination one could devise a role-play to at least reinforce learning in almost any area.

The most obvious uses of role-play are in those areas which deal primarily with aspects of communication. Role-play is a highly verbalized procedure, indeed one of the criticisms aimed against it is that it depends too much on linguistic ability. It is therefore ideally suited to those subjects which deal with linguistic ability, namely languages, literacy and social skills training. The incentive to take part in a role-play is high and, by taking part, one is using language and other ways of communicating so that learning is an integral part of the task. By devising scenes of everyday life, in particular those situations which make use of the vocabulary to be learnt, the student can be encouraged to use language in a free and interesting way. The development of linguistic skills need not be restricted to foreign languages; the technique is equally applicable to the improvement of spoken English.

> **HINT** Try a role-play between people from different social classes, age groups or cultures. Then analyse what the role-players used as key differences in language. What is 'good' English then?

Role-playing is ideally suited to enable students to learn new roles, become more aware of their own roles and understand more clearly other people's points of view. It is a highly appropriate technique for social skills training not only because of its ability to sensitize in this way, but also because of the way in which direct information on how to deal with certain situations and with officialdom can be incorporated into the scenario. Thus it is becoming increasingly important in the teaching of life skills.

There is a group of subject areas, namely history, sociology, literature, art, religion and politics, which deals in part with the way people live and the effect which people have on one another and their environment. Role-play can be used in these cases to give a picture of what life was like in the past, or how it is lived in different societies today.

This use concentrates on reproducing a picture of society. By using a more active form of role-play such as a public meeting, facts and figures may be bandied around and arguments exchanged on the merits of different ideas. In this way role-play can be used to demonstrate the importance of those areas of geography, science and natural history which impinge on people's lives; a use which is of particular relevance in view of the increasing concern over environmental matters.

One of the commonest uses of role-play takes the form of the interview. A straightforward use of this can be found on management courses where it is used to teach students the skills of interviewing, or in careers lessons where it teaches candidates how to present themselves at interviews. Similarly, the technique can be applied to the training of interviewers in television, radio or press, and conversely for the training of their 'victims'. The interview technique is also part and parcel of the skills needed by the 'helping' professions – social workers, doctors and psychologists among them. In many cases these professionals can also benefit from the use of role-play to help them empathize with the people with whom they deal. Such an exercise requires role-players to discuss questions 'as if' they were X, Y or Z. It encourages them to acquire a greater sensitivity to the total needs of their clients (Cooper, 1972).

Another use of role-play in management training lies in the fields of interpersonal skills, group dynamics and decision-making. There are many group exercises which require the participants to take decisions or reach a consensus whilst acting the part of key figures. These group development exercises can also be used in other situations where people have to be trained to work together as a team. Examples include research or project groups or teaching teams. This is an area where role-play may help even the 'hard' sciences or engineering disciplines.

The last specific area is that of negotiation. The setting up of a round-the-table negotiation may be used to explore the balance of resources in the Third World, the problems of international trade, the dilemmas of the philosopher or (of course) the actual skills of negotiation, whether as salesman, trade unionist or manager.

The use of role-play is widespread in management training because it enables the trainer to tackle the human side of the organization. Problems can and do arise in a number of areas, namely:

- power and authority;
- morale and cohesion;
- norms and standards;
- goals and objectives;
- change and development.

It can be seen that these topics can be readily incorporated into role-play scenarios.

Age groups

The technique of role-play can be used over a very wide age range. Children of five use it naturally as part of their games and it can be carried over into the classroom without any trouble. The author has used it with people in their 60s who were members of a local residents' group and with training counsellors of all ages. The hazards to be overcome differ with the various age groups.

The only problems that are likely to present themselves with the very young are those due to a lack of life experience. This means that there is little to draw on in the way of analogies and conclusions. The width and depth of experience will regulate the amount that can be drawn from the role-play.

A similar deficiency is likely to remain in the next age group, ten to 14 or thereabouts. In this case it can be overcome by a more comprehensive briefing. During the role-play itself the teacher may have to curb overenthusiasm but this is scarcely to be regarded as a fault, rather as a virtue of the technique. Debriefing for this group is likely to suffer from quick and divergent thinking and it may be wise to encourage students to pause for thought and to practise some convergent thinking in depth. The students may also find the change from emotional involvement to objective analysis difficult to handle.

TIP Use a symbolic object to denote 'in' or 'out' of role-play – when the box or jug is on the desk it symbolizes that 'acting' has finished and 'discussion' has begun.

The teenager is probably the most difficult person to work with, and at the same time the most rewarding. The typical symptoms of embarrassment at that age are likely to come to the fore and tutors should be prepared to carry out extended warm-up exercises until they are sure that self-consciousness has to a large degree been overcome. The teenagers want to see the relevance of what they are doing and the best role-plays for this group are tied into real problems which they can recognize and identify with. The debriefing session for this age group can be penetrating and in depth; the only limitation is the capacity of the particular group or tutor. One of the problems which is likely to present itself with this group (and those either side of it) is the dislike of doing anything which smacks of the childish. After all they are doing their best to 'put childish things away'. A careful, thoughtful briefing and warm-up is indicated.

! WARNING !

Discussion with teenagers can swing between personal and anecdotal evidence and sweeping generalizations. Ask for evidence and focus on general principles.

It is invidious to divide people's ages into bands, but the next group is what one might call young adults. (The exact boundary between child, teenager and young adult varies of course with the circumstances and the individual.) The relationship with the tutor can be important at this age because in an unconventional setting like role-play the boundaries of authority are not at all clear and the student needs to feel trust on both sides of a delicate relationship. On the other hand there is considerable scope for creativity since the young adult will be entering into a world of work and long-term responsibility which opens up new horizons to be explored. There are many issues to be argued, experienced and settled. It is perhaps possible at this age to see that everything is of some relevance to everything else, so that direct relevance is not as important as the feeling that the exercise is at heart a serious one and does not trivialize the issues.

The term middle-aged covers a wide spectrum of the population and most of the students on post-experience vocational courses will fall into this category. As with other age groups, they need to see the relevance of what they are doing to their jobs or problems. It is this group which shows more than most the division into those who take a conservative attitude to the way they want to be taught, and those who are eager and willing to try new methods. One can only hope that there are enough of the latter to carry the former along, otherwise the tutor is best advised to regard it as a challenge and failing that to just give a lecture instead!

TIP Show participants how much they've learnt in the past from experience rather than from lectures or books.

The use of role-play with the elderly does not present half the problem that one might imagine. The important thing is to take into account a general slowing up in reactions. This means taking a little more time to introduce the idea and certainly more time to allow students to prepare their roles. Obviously scenarios where the players are expected to react quickly have to be avoided. The debriefing session should be structured carefully so as to help students to memorize anything that they are required to. In this connection the use of teaching aids such as notes on a blackboard, or the use of flip-chart sheets to record ideas can be of great value and the tutor must always be prepared to slow things a little if the situation seems to demand it. Old age, like the need for glasses, creeps up on us imperceptibly.

Although not strictly related to age, it is relevant to comment here upon the use of role-play with disadvantaged or low income persons. At first sight the highly verbal nature of role-play (a point raised again in Chapter 6) militates against such people. It has been pointed out, however, that there are four reasons why role-playing may prove more congenial to them than other teaching techniques.

● It uses physical action, concrete example, problem orientation and flexible tempo.
● It reduces the distance between the professional and the disadvantaged individual.
● It is less office-ridden, bureaucratic and impersonal than traditional methods.
● It encourages verbal skills in an informal way.

Training and development of tutors

Although the use of role-play puts a powerful tool in the hands of the trainer or educator, it is a tool which requires much more skill and care than most educational techniques. It makes especial demands on the tutor's sensibilities and receptivity since there must be a constant interplay between student and tutor so that the right environment is created.

As with most skills, some people are born with a greater innate ability than others but they can improve their performance through proper training. Most people have a reasonable capacity for interacting with others and reacting to the needs of a situation; with the right course of training and development most people can run role-plays very successfully. The competence which is required can be broken down into three aspects.

- A thorough knowledge of the methodology.
- Sensitivity to individual and group behaviour.
- Self-knowledge, maturity, balance.

Methodology

As far as a knowledge of the methodology is concerned, reading books such as this one is clearly a big step in the right direction. Other books are listed in the reference section at the end of the book and there are articles to be perused both in simulation and gaming journals and in professional journals for industrial trainers, teachers, and groups such as nurses, youth leaders and those concerned with the education of adults in developing countries.

In reading them one must be wary of a trap. It is inevitable when writing to give the impression that one's advice is to be taken precisely and literally. The subtleties of inexactitude, of broad generalization, of areas of greater or lesser certainty are difficult to convey with the written word. Every author wants to express himself clearly, but this often means a false precision and air of certainty. By all means learn from the experience of others, but do not regard their words as gospel. They are written on paper, not tablets of stone. To take, choose and fashion to one's own requirements is the best approach.

There is a limit of course to the amount that can be learnt from the printed page. The rest must be acquired by practical means. The most important thing is to study the way in which other role-play organizers work and to try and see how the experienced facilitator organizes role-play. Even better than studying the operation from the outside is taking part oneself and no one should let such an opportunity go by. There are often occasions when small parts can be taken in order to help a colleague, and this enables one to study the process from the inside which is invaluable.

Observing how others direct role-play and taking part in their activities is one way of learning – trying out one's own skill is another. There are two ways in which this can be done without running the risk of failure with a group of students. The first is to try out simple role-plays or parts of more elaborate ones using a group of colleagues as guinea pigs. The other is to direct some role-plays under the supervision of a more experienced tutor. The first method is also useful when trying to develop new ideas and when writing new role-plays; the latter is a good way of regenerating one's energies and getting ideas for new approaches.

TIP Don't forget family and friends when looking for guinea pigs.

Individual and group behaviour

The idea of self-improvement and training is usually one which people view with a certain amount of trepidation and the effort is only sustained by a virtuous feeling of self-righteousness. The process of sensitizing oneself to individual and group processes, however, is one which can be pursued with interest and enjoyment. Opportunities present themselves at every turn and the learning cycle is continuous.

Whenever one is with a group of people who have a task to perform – a committee, a working party, a public meeting – there is usually an opportunity to stand back for a moment to observe the way the group members are interacting. The observation can be a general one, for example whether the group is sticking to the subject, whether the arguments are logical, whether one or two people are dominating the discussion. Alternatively a system of analysis can be used. Various systems have been suggested, some of which are discussed in Chapter 5, but it is equally acceptable to compile one's own. The idea is to become aware of the effects and implications of each contribution rather than the actual words that are spoken.

In a similar way it is possible to stand back momentarily from interactions with individuals and to ask oneself what the purpose of their remarks is, or to observe others together and question the emotional, the affective content of their dialogue.

Lastly, it is important to study the actions and words which comprise role behaviour in others. What is it about the voice, the intonation of a clergyman or naval officer which makes us identify them as such? What differences in dress or behaviour mark out the police officer when he is on or off duty? Can one recognize the farmer, the shopkeeper, the teacher, the writer by their mannerisms or behaviour? If so, when and how do these signals work? How universal or individual are they?

> **TIP** Another way of studying people's behaviour is to see or read the plays of an experienced dramatist such as Alan Bennett.

Having made the case for observing the behaviour of others in order to sensitize oneself to the nuances of their speech and actions, let me issue two warnings. The first is to get priorities right. The most important thing is to take part in group activities, to help make decisions, to establish good human relationships with others. The observation and analysis of other people's behaviour must always take second place to the business of living constructively and in harmony in the real world. The person who persistently 'opts out', who always stands on the side-lines, who observes but never takes part, who comments on the foibles of others but is never willing to risk exposing his own, is an abomination. We all recognize the amateur psychologist who stands aloof at parties and attempts to distance himself from the masses by analysing their foolish, human behaviour. Observe, note, analyse, but acquire the ability to do so considerately, as an almost unconscious memorization for recollection and learning afterwards.

```
┌─────────────── ! WARNING ! ───────────────┐
│                                            │
│  Don't cut yourself off by always acting as observer and critic. And   │
│  don't assume you see things the way others do.                         │
│                                            │
└────────────────────────────────────────────┘
```

The second warning is not to assume that because you have labelled a response as 'supportive', 'aggressive', 'information seeking', 'authoritarian', 'flight from task' or whatever, it will be seen as such by others. By all means interpret but do not deceive yourself that your interpretation is necessarily correct or that it accords with the way others perceive the situation. Whenever you have the opportunity check your perceptions by asking those involved how they saw the situation, what they felt about the discussion. It is not always possible to do this of course, but it is essential to correct one's impressions periodically to avoid building castles of interpretation in the air.

Self-knowledge

Those who organize and control role-play exercises put themselves in an unusual position in relation to their students – they are handing over part of the responsibility for the direction of learning to the student. But this very freedom to express themselves also puts students in a position where they may unwittingly expose their feelings and susceptibilities. The tutor has the responsibility and power to control the extent to which the student's involvement is used creatively or destructively. In these circumstances the tutor who is immature, lacks integrity or is unaware of personal weaknesses or biases is a liability. Tutors must therefore endeavour to take responsibility for checking their own self-knowledge.

Essentially the easiest way to do this is to participate in one of the many group experiences which are available nowadays. They go under a number of headings: sensitivity training, Outward Bound, encounter group, gestalt and others. What they have in common is an environment in which each member of the group is given feedback by the others on how his behaviour affects them, how he comes over to them. What is also necessary is a supportive framework in which the group member receives help and support from the others. This is more commonly found in encounter and gestalt groups than in T-groups or sensitivity training.

The problem is finding a group in which one can allow the natural barriers to self-exposure to fall and yet feel safe and secure. There is no simple answer to this and one must always take the responsibility of withdrawing from groups if the experience turns out to be too traumatic or destructive. The most that one can say is that research tends to indicate that the name of the group work, the label which it has been given, does not matter a great deal. What is important is the maturity, stability, personality, experience and skill of the group facilitator. A good group leader runs good groups.

But is all this really necessary? Well, strictly speaking, no. All that you need are friends who are sufficiently perceptive to see the effects of your actions, sufficiently honest to tell you, and sufficiently warm and concerned to support you if the information is hurtful. The essential thing is to have a mirror which will tell you the truth and, at the same time, the friendship of someone who will help you accommodate to the image that is revealed and possibly change it for the better.

Summary

Role-play is best used in teaching where the tutor wants students to experience and become involved in the situation they are studying and to formulate their attitudes towards it. It is an excellent way of developing interpersonal and communication skills and provides highly motivating and memorable lessons. It is therefore more suited to teaching in the social sciences and humanities and indeed in any area where human interaction is paramount.

The main problems in its use are the amount of time it can take and the reduction of the tutor's control over what is learnt. It is a powerful technique which, like any other tool, can be misused. The onus is on responsible tutors to ensure that they have the skills and ability to use the technique in a sensitive way. Age should not be a problem either for tutor or student.

It is part of the duty of an author to point out snags and difficulties. The fact remains that using role-play is basically both simple and enjoyable. The only requirement is that it is done in a thoughtful way, and the next chapter gives some ideas on how to do this.

3 *The systematic approach*

Like any tool or technique, there are good and bad ways of using role-play. One of the aspects of role-play which all users and investigators seem agreed upon is its immense power. Once the student is drawn in the psychological pressures can be considerable and this powerful force must be directed with skill and understanding in order to ensure the required result. Although the technique is relatively simple and one that most teachers and trainers can use without much prior experience, the difference between the best and worst run role-plays can be considerable. At best the exercise will be seen as a relevant, essential part of learning; it will be an enjoyable and exciting experience and the students will be left with a greater understanding of their subject and a clear idea of how to develop it further. At worst the students will be bored, embarrassed and even angry. They may have achieved very little and even acquired erroneous learning; they may be left with a feeling of inadequacy and not knowing what it was all about.

In order to get the best out of the use of role-play, therefore, the tutor should follow a procedure which ensures that each aspect is checked and used in the best way.

Figure 3.1 shows a flow chart for using role-play which performs different functions at different times. For the beginner it gives a logical sequence which ensures that each point is considered before too many assumptions are made. As the tutor becomes used to using the technique this sequence will become semi-automatic and there will no longer be a need to refer to the diagram. When one reaches the point of being jaded and nonchalant, however, it is time to refer back to the flow chart and check that every step in the sequence is receiving due attention.

Not all of the steps take an equal amount of time or resources.

Some of them require a chapter to themselves. What follows is a guided tour, as it were, to enable the reader to see the whole sequence in context.

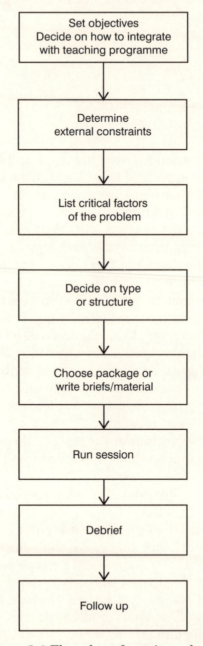

Figure 3.1 Flow chart for using role-play

Integrating into the curriculum

One must always start by asking oneself how the role-play is going to fit into the whole curriculum or timetable. Tutors must ask themselves why they have chosen to use role-play and what it is they expect to teach; is it facts, concepts, skills and techniques, awareness or sensitivity?

There are a number of ways in which a role-play may be fitted into the overall curriculum. Some of these are listed in Figure 3.2.

Introduction to the subject
Natural follow-up to a point being explored
Central feature of the course
Warm-up/break/interlude
Revision
Assessment

Figure 3.2 Functions of role-play in the curriculum

Subject introduction

Role-play may be used as a means of stimulating the imagination and opening up a subject. For example, it is possible to arrange a role-play in which a series of management levels are represented, together with specialist advisers or other outside influences. The exercise may be set up so as to involve communication between the various levels and other groups. A role-play of this type will illustrate many of the problems of management in ensuring good communications, and provide a basis for further teaching and discussion of the problem.

Another example of the use of role-play in introducing an involved subject and emphasizing its complexity would be the role-playing of a committee whose job it is to decide on the future of a child from a broken home. The possible alternatives such as leaving the child at home, putting into care, fostering, etc can be put before the committee in such a way as to leave the decision as finely balanced as it often is in real life. The difficulty of making such a decision will bring home to the participants the fact that such choices are not as simple or black and white as they may appear to the layman.

The door is then open to build on this with lessons on moral decisions, the structure of society, the needs of children, the role of the professional and so on.

Follow-up

Another common use for role-play is as a means of supplementing or following on from a point which is being explored. Suppose for example that a group of line supervisors are discussing a case study involving a breach of the health and safety regulations in force at their factory. One of the supervisors suggests pointing out the 'error of their ways' to the culprits. Another disputes the efficacy of that approach. A third is concerned about the possible side-effects of such an approach. It is easy to set up a role-play on the spot to explore the subject. The students already know the situation and the key facts; all that is needed is a gentle push in the right direction and a role-play can be set in motion.

Very often the role-play focuses attention on the effects of broad issues on individual people. If the class is dealing with a historical event such as the laws against the use of child labour in factories, it may be revealing to explore the effects on the individual family and in particular to expose the fact that reform can bring problems in its train for the individual on whose behalf the reformers are working. Again it enables the tutor to show different aspects of the subject and to stimulate interest and questions.

Centrepiece

The format of a public inquiry or public meeting is very useful and one of its uses is to act as a central focal point for a course. The course may be on Charlotte Bronte's novel, *Jane Eyre*. Apart from the purely literary or linguistic aspects of the novel the tutor may want to set it within the current concerns of mid-nineteenth century England, or more particularly the concerns of someone living in the West Riding of Yorkshire at that time. A possible approach would be to plan the course around a central set piece, a public meeting in Haworth (where the Brontes lived) to discuss the state of the roads, the coming of the railway, the impact of the cotton and wool industries and their mills. There would be many viewpoints which would be represented by the clergy, the millowners, workers, villagers, magistrates, shopkeepers and so on. The material for the meeting would both feed out of, and into, readings of the novel and other contemporary literature. It would give a focal point for work in the first part of the course and a reference point for the latter part.

A more obvious way of using the public meeting format as a centrepiece is within present day studies. It has been used to examine conflicting interests in the redevelopment of land, planning of motorways, siting of factories. One simulation uses an inquiry into the building of a power station as a means of motivating students to carry out the calculations needed to make comparisons between different forms of fuel.

Break

Not every use of role-play need itself result in learning. The motivating power of role-play can be used for its own sake to provide a break from the routine of the classroom or workshop. There is nothing wrong in recognizing that the creation of a suitable environment for learning is as important a task as any other for the tutor. Provided it is recognized as such, there is no reason why a role-play should not serve the purpose of relaxing tension, changing direction, establishing a different atmosphere in the classroom or different relationship between teacher and taught.

Summary

All too often in modern education students are taught a series of disparate subjects from different teachers. They may never realize that what is being taught is all part of a world which is interconnected. Because teaching, even sometimes in industrial training, is subject-and not problem-oriented the student only sees the parts and not the whole. A role-play can be used to review and integrate diverse material. By focusing on a problem, it is possible to demonstrate the way in which subjects interact.

The examples given above may be used for this purpose; alternatively another well-tried scenario is to cast the role-players in the characters of key people who have to defend their point of view in order to gain resources or to avoid defeat. A possible use of this in a physics course, for example, might be to cast students in the roles of various famous physicists and ask them to show how their discoveries had been of benefit to mankind. The same treatment could be used in looking at industry by asking students to take the roles of workers in different parts of the firm and to argue their value to the total enterprise. This would have the effect of showing the inter-dependence of people when they are at work.

> **TIP** When deciding on the roles to use, consider including a role in the local community to make players aware of the impact of their decisions on others.

Revision

It is a common experience that revision is one of the most boring activities in education and training. On the other hand role-play is one of the most motivating activities. It is only common sense, therefore, to consider putting the two together. The exact way in which this is done must depend on the particular circumstances, but with a little ingenuity it should be possible to introduce an element of role-play together with an element of competition also.

Assessment

Role-play is not normally used for assessment purposes in school or college. It is, however, a tool which has been used for many years in large firms, the armed forces and the civil service. Its main use is to assess candidates in situations of complexity and where group interaction is an important element. The main part of this book is concerned with teaching and training; a comment on the use of role-play in assessment will be found in Chapter 9.

These then are some of the ways in which role-play may be integrated as part of a complete teaching strategy. Wherever possible the students should be made aware of the way in which the session fits into the picture and, in the case of adults, should certainly be given an opportunity to be involved in the design and setting of objectives. As noted elsewhere, students should particularly be brought into consultations about the aspects to be observed and recorded.

It is also important in some cases to involve students' superiors, colleagues or employers in order to ensure the fullest support for any changes which the students may want to work at. In a book of this size it is impossible to go into detail about the particular support which may or may not be needed. The sensitive and aware tutor will ensure that the needs which may be created by changes in attitude or motivation arising from the role-play have been properly thought through.

Objectives

It may not always be possible to define objectives clearly, and in many cases what is learnt may differ from the original intention of the organizer. However, the tutor must at least be aware of the dangers of going into role-play without having thought of the relationship of the session to what has come before, or to what may follow.

The objectives of a session can be thought of either in instrumental terms, ie 'by the end of the session the student will be able to. . .', or in problem terms, ie 'during this session we will explore the problem of ... .' If the latter approach is used it leads naturally to a consideration of the broad scenario. Are we investigating industrial relations, prejudice, salesmanship, interview technique, environmental pollution, hospital management, or what? What sort of a scenario are we painting? Is it the whole world, one country, a village, a family, two people or part of one person?

HINT Discuss objectives, expectations and responsibilities with participants beforehand. Initial misunderstandings are a common cause of failure.

External constraints

The development and running of a role-play can be very time-consuming and it is important not to waste time on developing an exercise which in the event cannot be used. It is useful to consider at an early stage the factors which may inhibit or even completely prevent the running of a role-play.

The most important consideration is probably that of a suitable room or space in which to operate. A tiered lecture theatre is an almost certain recipe for disaster. One cannot get sensible multiple role-plays going since the students are in the wrong physical relationship to one another. If a demonstration role-play is run at the front of the room, the tiered seating emphasizes the theatricality of the occasion and puts unnecessary pressure on the role-players. Although inexperienced tutors should avoid using a tiered room it is not a complete impossibility; it does however call for confidence on the part of both tutor and class and a willingness to transcend physical limitations.

Ideally the room used for the role-play activities should be different from the normal classroom so that the change of surroundings helps set a different atmosphere. It is easier for the tutor's role to be seen as different if the physical aspects of the space are distinctly different from those to which the student has grown accustomed.

The ideal room is flat-floored and square-shaped rather than long and narrow. Size is not critical but a good area to work in would be one of between 70 to 100 square metres (750 to 1000 square feet). This gives a flexibility which enables a whole range of role-plays to be run – from duologues to public meetings – without losing the intimate atmosphere that is desirable. The minimum space for an interview with observers is about 20 square metres (215 square feet); over 200 square metres (2150 square feet) is getting to a point where some of the audience will feel remote from the action unless the class has been split into smaller groups.

The furniture should be moveable and preferably stackable. This enables various spaces to be cleared and shapes to be created. It is useful to have a few different types of chairs and tables, particularly if different settings are to be used in the same role-play.

HINT Introducing some artifacts, such as a vase of flowers, or moving the furniture around, will change the perceived environment.

Ceiling height is not usually a matter over which tutors are likely to have control but it is worth mentioning that the combination of a low ceiling in a small room will almost certainly lead to problems if smoking is to be allowed, whilst high ceilings in large rooms can make things inaudible, particularly if the role-players have quiet voices. The tutor must remember that, depending on the scenario, the role-players will not necessarily be projecting in the same way that a teacher does. Since the tutor will want to ensure as little inter-ruption as possible it is desirable for the room to be soundproof and subject to as little distraction as possible.

Equipment and materials are unlikely to be constraints but time almost certainly will be. There must be sufficient time available to warm up and brief the players, run the role-play and debrief again. It is sometimes desirable to have enough time to repeat all or part of the role-play with variations. On the other hand role-plays need not be lengthy in themselves. A simple role-play may last five to ten minutes, the majority between ten and 20 minutes although some of the more elaborate ones may continue for 20 or 40 minutes. The time available need not be in one block. Three blocks corresponding to briefing, running and debriefing may serve the purpose. As a rough guide they should be of equal length or in the ratio 1:2:3 depending on the details.

Another constraint to be considered at an early stage is the avail-ability or otherwise of people to help run the role-play. Do you need extra tutors to help in briefing? Do you need trained observers? Will you want to use real interviewees? Are you going to use students or outsiders as the experts, the witnesses, the chairman? It is also important to plan for a certain amount of flexibility in numbers to take account of last minute illness or other reasons for withdrawal. The use of observers may help towards this.

After checking on the practical constraints, it is opportune to look back on the original objectives and the broad scenario which has been decided upon. Now is the time when objectives or scenario may need to be reconsidered in the light of available resources. When these issues have been settled one can look at the critical fac-tors and these will help to narrow down the role-play towards its final shape.

Critical factors

Although the outline of the problem may be clear, there remains the task of deciding on the actual situation to present to the role-players. It is helpful to consider the critical factors which enter the situation. These can be considered in terms of who is going to take part in making decisions or be affected by them, the critical issues to be debated, and the key communication channels which can be used.

If the problem area is that of industrial relations in the health service, for example, one could draw up a list of people who might be involved. Such a list would include the relevant government official, civil servants, hospital administrator, union representatives, doctors, nurses, patients. The scenario could be at government, regional, hospital, ward or individual level depending on what particular aspects one wishes to explore.

Drawing up a list of possible roles ensures that all possibilities are looked at. Similarly, drawing up a list of critical issues and key communication channels may be of considerable help. In the previous example one might include pay, working hours, strike action, emergency service, patients' deterioration, comparability and lines of authority as critical issues. Key communication channels might be staff meetings, union negotiations, board meetings, talks between patient and nurse, and so on. In customer care industrial training, the issues may be: how to approach a customer, dealing with complaints, handling aggression, legal constraints, getting agreement, finishing on an upbeat note.

If we take another example, that of smoking by young people, the list of roles might include the cigarette manufacturer, doctors, teachers, parents, youth leaders, young people, shopkeeper. The critical issues might include responsibility for health, cost of illness, freedom of action, taxation revenue, advertising, effects on others. The key communication channels could be advertisements, school contacts, family and friends.

The drawing up of these lists does not force the tutor into any one pattern; it offers the choice of a spectrum of activities and roles. Once the choice is made and it has been decided, for example, that the role-play will take place at home, between a young girl, her mother, her married sister, etc, then the next step will be to decide on the type or structure of the role-play to be used. Many authors and facilitators appear to assume that there is only one type of role-play, but different types demand different approaches to briefing, running and debriefing. This is often the reason why role-plays go wrong and accordingly the question of role-play types and their use has been given a chapter to itself (Chapter 4). It is enough to note here that the principal reason for considering the different types of role-play is to enable the tutor to control the students' emotional involvement and to avoid a situation where the role-play becomes more arousing, provocative or distressing than had been intended.

Choosing or writing the role-play

We have already seen the need to set about things in a systematic fashion. By this stage in the process the tutor will have spent some time considering the broad objectives of the exercise. Now is the time to convert these overall ideas into the detail of the role-plays itself.

In theory, there is a choice between buying or borrowing a ready-made role-play or writing one's own. In practice most role-plays are written for specific needs and to fit into particular course programmes. There are of course a number of published simulations both in the UK and the US which cover general subject areas such as vandalism, sexual attitudes, prejudice, assertiveness and industrial relations. Many of them are well thought out and are particularly useful for those who want an example to follow or something to use as an introduction. The writing of role-plays is not difficult, however, and once the tutor has decided on the subject material it is usually better to adapt an existing role-play or write a new one for oneself. This ensures that the background is familiar or at least comprehensible to the participants and that they can see the direct relevance of what they are doing to the particular job or problem that they are concerned with.

Running the role-play

Ideally, as all the textbooks say, one should pilot the material that one is going to use, preferably with a similar audience. This is the counsel of perfection. In practice the organization of a pilot run can be as time-consuming (or even more so) as the actual role-play itself. Moreover, it is usually difficult to get a set of guinea pigs who are similar to the target group. Often the best that you can do is to discuss it with one or two colleagues.

It cannot be too strongly stressed that any piloting of the exercise is better than none. Even if it is only a discussion with colleagues it is still worth trying out some of the critical aspects, perhaps the very beginning or a point at which new information needs to be fed into the action. A small amount of time going through one's plans with someone else may prevent a critical element going wrong and disrupting the whole role-play.

HINT Most people have a secret desire to be someone else for a few moments; they show this when telling a story or joke. Play on this.

Once the material has been prepared the running of the role-play itself will follow its own sequence of introduction, warm-up, running and ending. The main problem for the tutor at this point is the timing of the segments. In particular the ending of the role-play must be timed in such a way as to fit into the whole programme. This can be done either by writing the mechanism for ending into the role-play itself, 'You must have reached agreement on all five points before 11.30 when you have to attend a meeting of the board of directors', or by the tutor in role, 'I'm sorry to disturb you Mrs Johnson, but there's a visitor waiting outside who says that he can't wait much longer', or by the tutor as himself, 'I'd like to stop the action there so that we can consider some of the points that have been raised'.

Debriefing

! WARNING !

One of the most common mistakes in role-play is to misjudge the amount of time needed for debriefing.

The term 'debriefing' has come into being as a common term used by the military. Its original meaning was that of 'milking' the participants of the knowledge that they had acquired by taking part in a military operation. It is unfortunate that the term has entered into the vocabulary of simulation and gaming because it implies that the process is being carried out for the benefit of the tutor. There is an inference that debriefing is basically checking that the right lesson has been learnt and feeding information to the tutor.

It is much more in keeping with the spirit of role-play to regard this period as one of reflection in which the players are able to absorb and analyse the impact of new learning on themselves, or one of discussion in which the whole group draws out the new perceptions, knowledge and understanding that were embedded in the role-play.

In this book, however, the term 'debriefing' has been retained on the grounds that:

- it is the term most commonly used;
- the term 'reflection' lays too much emphasis on the process being an individual rather than a group one;
- the term 'discussion' conveys the sense of an unstructured session, whereas the debriefing session should be carefully structured to get the maximum effect.

Although the term 'debriefing' will be used, the reader should bear in mind that the true nature of the process is two-way, and it certainly does not have the overtones of authority or of disbanding the group which it had in its original usage.

Whatever term is used, there is no doubt that for many purposes it is the debriefing period which establishes the learning in the student's mind. It is at this point that the consequences of actions can be analysed and conclusions drawn. It is at this point also that mistakes and misunderstandings can be rectified. Most important of all, it is from well-conducted debriefing that one can proceed to draw out the implications of what the students have been experiencing and make plans for the continuation of their learning about the subject.

Follow-up

Just as we began by stressing the importance of considering the function of the role-play within the total curriculum, so we must consider the way in which the exercise will lead naturally into the next activity.

If the role-play has been used to teach a skill or rehearse a new situation then it is logical to repeat it until the necessary degree of competence has been reached. If its purpose was to raise questions, then the follow-up should be arranged to answer them. Sometimes the role-play will have been used to arouse an awareness of a subject or problem and the group may want to discuss how to proceed; at other times the role-play will act as the final part of a sequence of instruction, a summing up as it were.

Whatever the objectives of using role-play, one must always consider the connection between it and the next activity. Such activities may include writing an essay, further reading around the subject, formal lessons, further role-plays or simulations, or even putting into practice what has been learnt. The main thing is to avoid leaving the role-play activity in a vacuum.

By following a systematic route through the use of role-play, tutors are more likely to make efficient use of the time and resources available. More importantly perhaps, they will finish up near the point they aimed for and with fewer detours on the way.

4 Types of role-play

Basic categories of role-play

Most people writing or talking about role-play appear to assume that all role-plays are basically the same and that different writers or teachers are dealing with a single class of event. At best they prevent themselves from using the technique as effectively as they might by making this assumption; at worst they may find that their sessions fall to pieces or develop in capricious ways.

Role-play is a type of communication. Like other means of communication it can be used for messages, expressing or arousing emotion, negotiation and persuasion, or for a variety of other purposes. The words are the same – it is the intent which is different. Although tutors may not be consciously aware of the various types of role-play, they show from their actual instructions and the way they organize and administer their role-plays that they are subconsciously aware of the differences. Different types of role-play demand different approaches; the way in which the role-play is introduced, the description of roles, the facilitation and post-play analysis will all vary according to the type of role-play which is being used. If the wrong approach is used, or the tutor gets confused as to which type he is using, then the students can get mixed up and not receive the support they need.

A broad and important distinction may be made between those role-plays dealing with the practice of skills and techniques, and those dealing with changes in understanding, feelings and attitudes. Examples of the former might be the training of interviewers and salesmen where they are asked to rehearse a pattern of behaviour in a simulated situation. Examples of the latter might be an exploration of the implications of being a member of a minority group or an attempt to increase the student's understanding of the way in which groups behave, or the study of bargaining behaviour.

The essential point is that the conduct of the session must be adapted to the type of role-play used. If the first type (the skills development type) is used then the instructor will have to ensure that trainees have been given an outline of the correct way to approach the problem. The environment and role instructions will be carefully chosen to impose the constraints and problems likely to be encountered in the job. The trainee may well be put through a series of graded situations which aim to present a succession of problems. The debriefing will use the original framework given by the trainer to analyse the effectiveness of the trainee's performance. The trainee may have been told to use a certain form of words or to go through a sequence of actions for example; in this case the debriefing will include a check on whether this pattern was followed. Finally, trainees will often be offered a chance to repeat the exercise and improve their performance.

The conduct of the second type, intended to explore feelings and attitudes, is quite different. The initial introduction will be more concerned with describing the problem than offering a solution. The framework for the role-play itself will be less tightly constrained so as to allow the players more scope to involve themselves and use their own personalities and experience. During the running of the role-play different methods such as shadowing, 'alter ego' and group consultancy may be used to draw out special aspects. The role-play may become emotional as players are drawn into exploring their own and others' feelings. After the role-play has finished the tutor will spend some time probing the reasons for certain responses and will conduct a carefully structured debriefing to ensure that the students are brought back to reality and have no remaining worries about the way the role-play went.

These two broad categories may be subdivided to produce a list of six functions which a role-play can fulfil. This represents one way in which the range of role-plays can be categorized. The main part of the chapter will look at this particular classification which has been devised and used by the author. It has the virtue of distinguishing between differing requirements in the way of briefing, running and debriefing. These differing requirements stem largely from the distinctive ways in which the role-plays involve the role-player emotionally. It is therefore of considerable use in ensuring that the tutor does not find himself dealing with a role-play which has developed further into the realms of passion and sentiment than was at first intended. Other ways of categorizing role-plays will be discussed later in the chapter.

The six functional areas which comprise this categorization are listed down the left-hand side of the table in Figure 4.1. There is another dimension to the classification and that is the identity of the main role-players, or protagonists. The role-players are often, but not always, the students. They may, however, be playing themselves or other characters such as the student with whom they are paired or a character completely outside the classroom. Similarly, role-players may be the tutor or a person from outside the trainee group. This second dimension, that of the protagonist, is shown along the horizontal axis of the table.

Not every cell in the table represents a variant which is normally used but a brief phrase in each one indicates the image represented. Since these are abstract concepts they do not have the clear definition of a physical description but as long as readers recognize where their own particular role-play fits into the scheme this does not matter. Categorizing role-plays is not simply an academic exercise. Each category requires a different approach in briefing, running and in debriefing, and the notes below elaborate on this. The table is arranged in a rough order of involvement. Categories at the bottom and to the left offer the most degree of involvement, those at the top-and to the right the least.

A. Describe

In this category the role-play is being used as a means of communication to describe a situation which can be more graphically illustrated by means of dramatization than by pure verbal description.

A tutor may wish to illustrate how it is difficult to avoid an escalation when one of the protagonists takes an uncompromising line. He does this by taking the role of a shop steward and one of the trainees takes the part of the manager or a shop floor worker.

Two teenagers may want to show their youth group how they see the problem of parental control in a typical situation. One of them may take the role of a daughter asking if she can stay out late, the other the part of one of her parents. Similarly a student may re-enact how he tried to ask his boss for a rise; alternatively he may

Function / Protagonist		Student(s) playing			Tutor	Outsiders
		Self	Other student	Outside people		
A	DESCRIBE To *illustrate*, demonstrate problem/ situation/ process	A1 Look, this is how I see the situation.	A2 Is this the situation you found yourself in?	A3 This is how that type of person behaves.	A4 Let me show you what the situation is.	A5 This is our situation.
B	DEMONSTRATE To demonstrate *technique*	B1 This is how I do it.	B2 This is how you might do it.	B3 They use this method.	B4 Let me show you how to deal with this situation.	B5 This is how we would handle the situation.
C	PRACTISE To practise *skill*	C1 I'll try to improve the way I do this.	C2 I'll copy what you show me.	C3 We'll improve our technique by putting ourselves in this situation.	C4 You can practise on me.	C5 You can practise on us.
D	REFLECT To give *feedback*	D1 I take a look at myself from within.	D2 This is how you appeared to me.	D3 Now I understand the reasons for their behaviour.	D4 This is how you appear to others.	D5 This is how you appear to us.
E	SENSITIZE To increase *awareness/ sensitivity* of situation/ others	E1 Now I feel more conscious of my feelings.	E2 Is this the effect I have on you?	E3 Now I understand what others must feel like.	E4 Lend me your ears.	E5 Documentary drama.
F	CREATE/ EXPRESS	My actions express my feelings.				

Figure 4.1 Types of role-play

enact a situation described by another student to ensure that he understands it properly.

This category is very close to that of drama. Indeed it overlaps with improvized 'street theatre' or 'educational drama'. In both cases the plot and key points of the dialogue will be agreed beforehand. The participants may well have rehearsed their approach, at least in their minds, and unlike conventional theatre the intent is to start a discussion and other educational activities. One can imagine a group of students dramatizing the conflict between landowners and peasants in the eighteenth century, prior to the large-scale enclosures in England, as part of a classroom simulation during a history lesson, or the same situation being portrayed by professional actors. The difference is in what the role-players do for a living, their technical skills as actors and how they perceive their role, whether as student or actor.

The implications are that there is little emotional involvement on the part of the role-players. They need to have an understanding of the situation and the briefing if any will concentrate on the facts of the situation. There will be no need for observers as such and the first stages of debriefing may be restricted to correcting any factual errors before going straight into a discussion or other activity using the subject presented.

B. Demonstrate

There is considerable similarity between this category and the previous one, but the intention here is to give a demonstration which may be copied by the student. It is what the social psychologist would call a role-model. The salesman demonstrating how to close a sale with a client, the social worker showing a parent how to play with a child, the psychologist illustrating how to deal with aggression, or the language teacher exemplifying the use of a particular phrase structure in a realistic scene, are examples of this category.

Here again the emotional involvement is minimal. The attention centres on the technique being demonstrated or depicted and role-players will not usually need briefing since they are portraying an action with which they are familiar. The most common arrangement is where tutors are carrying out demonstrations themselves; in this case it is likely that the students will be briefed as observers so that they know what to look for and which points to watch.

The debriefing session should provide no problems except to

ensure that the students are capable of discriminating between the critical actions of the model. It should be possible to draw a list of such actions out in discussion with the students.

C. Practise

The previous two uses of role-play are relatively rare, at least in their pure form, although we will see that they often appear as part of other types of role-play. This kind is much more common. Typical situations are where a young person is practising social skills; students are trying their hand at using a foreign language in a practical context; managers, counsellors, police officers are developing their various interviewing skills; teachers, salesmen or psychiatric nurses are improving their ability to communicate with their students, customers or patients.

Preparation for this class of role-play must be detailed and meticulously carried out. Obviously the student must be clear about the task to be performed. There must be some guidance on how to do the job, such as a list of do's and don'ts, a set of procedures or sequence of instructions. This initial framework will also be used to direct the observers and to act as a check on how the student performs.

A simple sequence of instructions for a practice interview, for example, might go as follows: 'Put the interviewee at their ease; check that the factual information on the form is correct; explore their reasons for applying for the job; tell them something about the job re-check that their reasons for applying and their past achievements tally with the job requirements; give the candidate an opportunity to ask any final questions; tell them when they will hear from you and by what means; thank them for coming'.

HINT It helps to write down beforehand the instructions you intend to give. This avoids errors and omissions.

The observers would be given this list and asked to ensure that each of the stages was gone through and, if necessary, in the correct order. Part of the debriefing would then consist of the tutor and observers checking back with students as to how they performed in relation to the list of actions which they were supposed to have carried out. In addition, the observers and tutor may well wish to comment on the extent to which role-players achieved their objectives in terms of, eg, putting the interviewee at ease or finding out about a particularly sensitive period in his or her life. In doing this they will probably be helped by the fact that most role-plays of this type involve a second actor who plays the part of the interviewee, customer, patient or whoever is needed in the particular context. This secondary player will be able to provide direct feedback on the extent to which they were put at ease or enticed into revealing delicate information, etc.

As can be seen, although the main intention of this category of role-play is to rehearse a predetermined sequence of actions and although the tutor can make the process as objective as possible, an element of emotional risk-taking has come into the scene. The student is being asked to perform a task in public, and this performance is being observed and criticized. Moreover, there are some role-play situations in which one of the critics will be a person who, in another role, has 'suffered' as a consequence of the student's lack of adroitness. The reality and degree of this 'suffering' will vary of course with the realism with which the role-play is staged, but even in the simplest arrangement there will be an element of touchiness about the situation.

The tutor can control the degree of emotional feeling engendered by the role-play by the extent to which the situation is circumscribed and the specific instructions which are given to the role-players. Clearly the process of buying a railway ticket is not in itself an emotional task; if the person playing the part of the railway clerk is told that he is hard of hearing, or dislikes the racial group or religious sect of the protagonist, then a certain amount of emotion will be generated. Conversely, breaking the news of a fatal accident will normally be a traumatic experience but by carefully taking the learner through a series of graded exercises and then giving him a detailed method of approach, the training session may be made acceptable. It is the unstructured and the unexpected which cause the greatest emotional upset.

So far we have tended to ignore the horizontal dimension of Figure 4.1. When we are talking about the use of role-play for description or demonstration it does not greatly matter who is doing the describing or demonstration. As we go down the table, however, we will find that the differences between the left- and right-hand sides become more significant. In the case of the practice function of role-play, the part played by the student must necessarily be different to that played by the tutor or outside person. In the case of the former he is carrying out the practising either (C1) by putting himself into a particular situation, such as ordering a meal, or (C2) by imitating the actions of another student of, say, another sex, age, racial group, or (C3) by putting himself in a role which he does not normally occupy, for example a manager, police officer, chairman, and using this as a device to help him learn a particular technique.

In the case of the tutor or outsider doing the role-playing we have the ubiquitous example of the dummy or surrogate patient on which student doctors, nurses or first aiders may practise. This is now so much part of training that in Britain a flourishing organization, the Casualties Union, exists with its own journal in which hints and tips on the role-playing of different types of casualty, including mental patients, are published. Much of the teaching in some university medical faculties centres round the use of simulated patients. Quite often, in a less formal way, a tutor will act as a substitute for the real thing when teaching students how to handle a particular situation.

One of the distinguishing features of the role-play used as a practice medium should be that the student is given the opportunity to have another go at the problem after having heard the criticism and suggestions of the observers and tutor. It is unfortunately one of the features acknowledged more in the breach than in the observance since all role-play activities suffer from a lack of time. Repeat opportunities are more likely to be seen in this type of role-play than in most others.

D. Reflect

The difference between this category and the previous one is more one of intent than action. The emphasis throughout is on observation and reflection. The easiest groups to describe are those on the right of the table which deal with the involvement of outside groups or the tutor. The objective of their role-playing is to show the student how his behaviour appears to others. In most cases this will probably consist of spontaneous demonstrations by means of a short piece of mimicry; sometimes the tutor or observers may be explaining their observations to the student and he will ask 'what do you mean?' This can be the cue for a brief example from the observer. More extended disclosure can best be achieved by the use of closed circuit television recording, although the performance of a dramatic sketch, often satirical, is another example of the use of role-playing to bring home to someone the impact of his behaviour.

The reflective role-playing of the student is more difficult to describe. It is in many ways similar to the straightforward practising of an approach or method of dealing with a situation but the emphasis is on a continuous analysis of what is being done and its effects on others. In addition to action, there is a lot of thinking going on. In the case of the role-play for practice purposes, the role-player is encouraged to concentrate on doing the job as efficiently as possible. He will concentrate on persuading the nervous mother to go to ante-natal classes, finding out as much as possible about the juvenile offender during an interview, putting across his point of view in a committee meeting. In the case of the reflective style of work, on the other hand, he will be instructed to be conscious of what he is doing, why he used the particular phrases he did, how a specific effect had been obtained.

The key difference is that students who use role-play for practice will need feedback on their performance in order to assess the degree of improvement. This feedback will concentrate on the extent to which they followed the 'correct' procedure as laid down by the instructor; the criticism will be concerned with why they were not following the set pattern.

On the other hand, the feedback on performance in the reflective mode will be continuous. The role-player is intensely introspective and the function of the tutor is to ensure that the student is able to look at himself as he performs the task. At the end of the role-play the debriefing will concentrate on the reasons why certain things were said rather than the effect they had, although naturally some attention is bound to be paid to the effects of the actions.

To illustrate the difference more clearly let us look at an example. A trainee accountant is attending a course for auditors. As part of this course he is asked to role-play the situation where he has to interview the head of a department about some petty cash payments and the voucher system of control. The person playing the head of the department makes him a tetchy person who is oversensitive to anything he sees as implied criticism. The trainee auditor is told that there are particular problems about those petty cash payments in which part or all of the payment has been repaid to the department directly instead of being refunded through the accounts section.

The instructions for a straight practice role-play might be as follows: explain to the manager why you are there; make sure that you get a complete list of the payments and their details; find out what procedures are followed in the case of refunds and the extent to which these are followed; ensure that the manager realizes the problems caused by sloppy procedures and finish by explaining to him that it will be necessary to come and see him again after you have had time to look at the vouchers in detail.

The instructions for the reflective role-play might be: your purpose is to gain the cooperation of the head of the department who, not unnaturally, will be on the defensive; during the interview ask yourself whether you are keeping his needs in mind when you ask your questions; check whether you are just seeking to impose your authority on him; verify the extent to which you are listening to him; establish whether you are going at the right pace.

The implications of these differences in the two approaches can be divided into those relating to the briefing phase, the playing phase and the debriefing phase. In the briefing phase the tutor running a practice session will give the student a clear set of instructions to work at. Apart from this there is no need for any preliminary training. In the case of the reflective session the student is given an overall objective rather than detailed instructions on how to handle the situation. The session needs to be preceded by some instruction and practice on using techniques of self-observation.

During the role-play itself the tutor will only interrupt the practice lesson if the student is going badly wrong and needs to be corrected on the way in which he is doing things. The tutor who is running a reflective type of role-play may interrupt in order to interpret what is going on or to ask the student to attempt an interpretation.

At the end of the practice role-play the debriefing should relate directly to the instructional framework which is being learnt. In the case of the reflective style of role-play the debriefing will centre on the observations of the role-players about their motivation and the reasons for their actions. This should normally lead on to a discussion of aspects of motivation and behaviour, and the ways in which it can be changed.

Although the general principle of role-play in training and education is that it is not a theatrical experience, it is possible in some circumstances to encourage the participants to be aware of themselves 'playing a part'. This is known as 'metaxis': a situation where participants feel simultaneously involved and detached from the situation they experience, and is explored in more depth by Collier (1998).

E. Sensitize

If there is a close relationship between practising and reflecting upon one's actions, so is there a relationship between introspection about one's actions and an awareness of one's feelings and emotions during a role-play.

Here again there is a distinct difference between the role-play types on the right of Figure 4.1 which are concerned with the playing of roles by the tutor or outsiders, and those to the left of the table which are concerned with the role-playing of the student himself. The acting of the tutor or outsider to arouse an awareness on the part of the student is in fact almost that, ie acting in the traditional sense. The outsider may be portraying a situation in order to emphasize the emotional content and to encourage the student to empathize with those caught up in the situation. The tutor may be using rhetoric to sway the students' feelings.

The sections relating to the student being in role imply a much more difficult and sensitive area. Indeed by definition we are now entering the field upon which many tutors fear, quite reasonably, to tread. It is also a field into which some tutors rush without realizing that they have passed through a boundary line.

The tutor (or facilitator, which is the more likely term in this type of role-play) tries to create an environment in which the student will allow any emotional feeling which is brought about by the interaction to surface. Just as poetry is emotion recollected in tranquility, so in this type of role-play emotion which has been stimulated during the session can be scrutinized and analysed afterwards. This enables the role-players to recollect the emotion, sensitize themselves to its appearance, and remember it on future occasions if they wish.

The scenario for this type of session varies from the relatively unthreatening role-play undertaken to sensitize oneself to the feelings of another person, to the highly charged and potentially threatening activities used in therapeutic groups. The dividing line is a thin one, and any tutor who instructs students to expand and examine their emotions must be aware of straying into potentially dangerous territory.

The key factor here is the extent to which the preplay instructions and post-play discussion dwell on the actual personality and being of the role-player himself. If the purpose of the role-play is clearly to become aware of the problems and points of view of others, whether by trying to take on their characteristics or by putting oneself (as oneself) in their environment, then any emotional feelings can be compartmentalized as belonging to the role-player when in role.

If on the other hand the emphasis is on the real idiosyncratic personality of the role-player himself and the emotional consequences of this in the role-play situation, then one is dealing with a therapeutic situation in which the intent is to change the personality of the student. Close questioning by the tutor or other observers on the emotional or hidden reasons for action is an indicator of this type of role-play.

The implications are obvious. If the tutor wishes to keep the role-play restricted to a normal educational or instructional milieu then he must limit the amount of probing which is anticipated or allowed to take place in the post-play discussions. For example, if the role-play has been about a black youth who is questioned by the police the post-play discussion might go something like this:

> *Tutor* 'How did you feel when he stopped you?'
> *Student* 'I felt frightened.'
> *Tutor* 'Why did you feel frightened?'
> *Student* 'Because he seemed to tower over me. I knew I hadn't done anything, but I felt I might say something wrong. I didn't know what was going to happen next.'

Up until this point the discussion is on the reaction of the student in role. Any worry or anxiety created by the discussion is therefore 'distanced' by the fact that we are discussing the emotions created within the role character.

> *Tutor* 'Have you ever felt like that in real life?'

Now we are getting on to more sensitive ground.

> *Student* 'Yes.'

At this point the tutor has a choice of probing into the student's personal life and emotional problems, or using the experience as a base from which to draw general lessons and follow-up points. Either:

Tutor 'Tell us more about the times when you had these feelings of fear when faced by authority. What is it that makes you feel that way?'

or ...

Tutor 'Why do you think that people have feelings of fear when faced by authority? Do you think that the fact that you were playing a black person made any difference? What changes could be made to avoid this situation?'

As in J M Priestley's play, *Dangerous Corner*, there is a point at which the naive or insensitive tutor can take the wrong turning unawares. The question always to ask is 'What is the purpose of the role-play? Am I trying to explore the hidden psyche of this student or the problem situation which we are studying?' The questions will then automatically tune themselves to probe either the person – with the possibility of getting into a therapeutic situation and all its attendant dangers – or the role character and situation which is the normal educational or training objective.

! WARNING !

Be careful about relating general points to participants' personal private life.

F. Create/Express

This category has been included for the sake of completeness. It is the basis of the creative drama movement and, as the heading indicates, is the specialized group of techniques used to encourage students to develop their creative self-expression through the medium of drama.

Summary

Figure 4.2 gives a summary of the principal types in this method of classification and indicates how the three principal phases of the session – briefing, play and debriefing – vary with the choice of type.

Figure 4.2 is set out in such a way that those functions which are closest to cognitive learning come at the top of the table whilst those which rely on affective elements come near the bottom. It is important that the students should realize at which end of this continuum they are working.

The two basic approaches

There are other schemes which have been put forward by various authors. Some of them take a similar approach to the classification of role-play, but simplify it to only two types. These are what Shaw (1980) calls structured and unstructured, and Wohlking (1980) calls method-centred and developmental.

In Shaw's structured role-play there are predetermined goals and relationships. The whole exercise is planned ahead to cover a particular situation and explore it in terms of the way that situation is structured. The constraints and conflicts are built into the roles so that the whole exercise is rather like a case study or problem in which there are one or more solutions to be found. The objective of the role-play is to resolve the conflicts or arrive at a compromise solution. In the unstructured role-play the objectives are more concerned with allowing the players to explore their own problems or situations. The action flows freely from the player's own knowledge and wishes and may take a variety of forms and directions. There is no predetermined end-point and the players continue until they have reached the point at which they want to stop.

Wohlking's categories are very similar. The method-centred role-play which corresponds to Shaw's structured category is designed to develop the players' skills in specific procedures, methods or techniques. It assumes that the session will deal with situations which consist of a series of short problems that can be dealt with by following the proper steps or procedures. The tutor will provide suitable guidelines for the student to follow and the whole thing can be repeated several times in order to learn the correct procedures to follow. Examples of the type of situation to which this sort of role-play might be applied are registering a new student or patient, ordering a meal at a restaurant, carrying out a financial transaction such as at a supermarket checkout or bank, or conducting a wedding service. This corresponds most closely to the 'Practise' function in Figure 4.2.

Function	Briefing of role-play	Play	Debriefing
Describe	Facts.	No observers.	Factual errors.
Demonstrate	None.	Observe critical aspects of technique.	Ability to discriminate critical aspects.
Practise	Instruction/ Procedures.	Observe whether procedure is followed. Repeat for further practice.	Check on procedures. Check whether objectives achieved. Feedback from antagonist.
Reflect	Give overall objectives. Teach techniques of self-observation.	Encourage consciousness of actions, motives. Stop if necessary.	Analyse reasons for behaviour.
Sensitize	Develop trust. Structure on role or role-player depending on purpose.	Interrupt only if emotionally desirable.	Probe role or person depending on purpose.
Create/Express	Develop trust and freedom.	Stimulate imagination.	None.

Figure 4.2 Summary of types and their implications

The developmental type, similar to Shaw's unstructured category, is concerned with learning about attitudes and motivations. It deals with relatively complex situations and is a process of integrating and applying learning from a variety of sources including the student's own background knowledge and experience. The behaviour of the role-players is spontaneous and not modelled on an example provided by the tutor. This type of role-play incorporates elements of the functions 'Reflect' and 'Sensitize' in Figure 4.2; it can be used to teach communication skills, negotiating and counselling skills, and to develop the skills of group leadership and group participation. It enables participants to experiment with different approaches and to study the processes which are in operation in meetings and group activities of all kinds.

These two basic types of role-play are themselves related to two types of educational process, the didactic and the discovery-oriented. Didactic education is characterized by a sequential presentation of data and information from a teacher or other resource. Discovery-oriented learning is characterized by a relative lack of structure and the development of insights by the student from material which comes from a variety of sources, including other students. To a large extent the student has control over the pace of learning.

Thus method-centred or structured role-play is analogous to the didactic approach, whilst the developmental or unstructured role-play parallels discovery-oriented learning. Other authors have identified these two basic types but have gone as far as to call the unstructured/developmental type 'role-plays' whilst labelling the structured/method-centred type 'simulation-games'.

Framework constraints

Another way of looking at different types of role-play is via the range of constraints which can be placed upon the framework or, in other words, the way in which the situation or roles are defined. One may consider a role being defined in one of a number of ways which are listed in Figure 4.3 and discussed below.

Of course most role-plays in practice will consist of a mixture of these types in varying degrees but for the sake of classification one can regard each category as being typified by a predominance of one particular aspect.

- Function, authority, power
- Objectives, motives, targets
- Background, context
- Skills or abilities
- Social expectations
- Personality traits

Figure 4.3 Framework constraints

Function, authority, power

Roles are given to people such as chairman, manager or parent. This establishes their position within the structure and their relationship to others. It may be done in an overt fashion as with the examples given, or in covert ways by allocating roles such as female, foreigner, which have an implicit position in the structure of some societies.

Objectives, motives, targets

In this case the roles are defined not in terms of the status or position of the role-players, but by the objectives which have been set for them. Thus, 'your role is to get the committee to argue to. . . ' or 'success depends on the extent to which you can. . .

Background, context

Sometimes it is sufficient to paint in the backcloth to the action, 'You are in a church, at a disco, watching a football match, going through customs...' The conventions and assumptions made in these circumstances can provide the material for the role-play without a lot more detail.

Skills or abilities

The part which is played by each individual may be defined by their particular knowledge, ability or skill. This may be indicated in the role-description by saying something like 'You are the expert on fish behaviour...', 'You will be able to show the operatives how to make...... You understand the culture of the. . . ' and by backing up the player with the necessary documentation.

Alternatively, the abilities of players may be indicated by a description of their age, background or experience. In this case the information which students put into the role-play will come from their own experience or imagination.

Social expectations

One of the ways in which roles are defined in real life is by the expectations which the role-title produces in others. The same mechanism may be used in role-play. Roles are given names much as in the game of Happy Families, 'You are Mr Bun the Baker', or 'You are Miss Plod the policeman's daughter'. The role-play equivalent would be 'You are a vicar's wife', 'You are a used-car salesman', 'You are a newspaper reporter'.

This method of defining roles has the advantage of being close to life but the same disadvantage that real role-taking has, namely that people's expectations of a role are hung around with preconceptions, prejudices and myths. After all, not all mothers-in-law are dragons, not every social worker wears jeans, many nurses are not even female and still less like the popular image that has been created of them.

Personality traits

This is the type of description which used to be popular when role-play first became widely used. It is still the method used by many tutors, particularly when they have a general idea of role-play as a technique but have not had the time or opportunity to explore the subject in depth.

A typical description under this heading would be 'You are a woman of about 45 who is rather aggressive towards younger people although gentle with older people. You have a good sense of humour and are very tidy. You cannot understand why so many teenagers indulge in premarital sex; you are sensitive to the needs of the disabled . . . ', or 'You are a man in your early 20s with a temper which is difficult to control. You are rather neurotic and have a strong dislike of animals. On the other hand you like children and are kind towards them. You are authoritarian at work but believe in democracy in marriage...'.

```
┌─────────────────┤ ! WARNING ! ├─────────────────┐
│                                                  │
│  Avoid defining a role by a list of personality  │
│  traits. Use one of the other methods (see also  │
│  Chapter 5 – 'Role briefs').                      │
│                                                  │
└──────────────────────────────────────────────────┘
```

This type of description gives great freedom to the literary ambitions of the author but also places burdens on the role-player along with other disadvantages which are discussed in the section of Chapter 5 dealing with the writing of role briefings.

The framework constraints have been expressed above in terms of the way in which the roles are defined. Another way of looking at the same thing is to consider the rules, whether expressed or implied, by which the role-play is being regulated. James Coleman (Boocock and Schild, 1968) has divided these rules into procedural rules, which mirror the activities and functions used in social interaction; behavioural constraints, which delineate the role obligations found in real life; individual goals, which to a large extent determine the framework of the role-play; environmental responses, which give the probable response of the environment to statistical events; and police rules, which spell out the consequences of breaking one of the role-play rules. Having determined the rules, one then regards each role-player as providing the social environment of the other players.

Characteristics

One way of classifying role-plays is by lists of defining characteristics such as the point in time in which they take place – past, present or future. The reader may draw up his own lists from some of the characteristics discussed in this book; there is no accepted definitive list. The examples given in Figure 4.4 will be useful in drawing up such a list.

Method

The different methods of actually running the role-play such as fishbowl, multiple, role-reversal, may be used as a way of classifying role-plays. A checklist of these methods is given in Figure 7.2, Chapter 7.

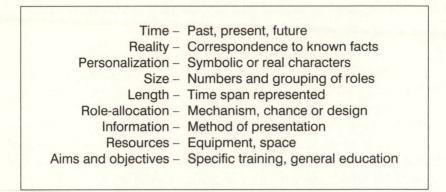

Figure 4.4 Defining characteristics

Using the classifications

At this point there may well be a number of readers who feel that the classification of role-plays is just an academic exercise designed to occupy those who do not have the desire or ability to run actual role-play exercises themselves. The theoretical value of classifying and categorizing cannot be denied. It is always important to establish the extent to which everyone is talking about the same thing, and a classification system helps to define the exact subject of discussion. Moreover, a taxonomy often suggests lines of research because it tends to show more clearly the connections between apparently different items.

HINT Thinking about classifications of role-play helps to generate ideas about writing and running them.

If these were the only functions of classifying, there would be little reason to have devoted several pages to a discussion of different ways of looking at the range of role-plays. There are at least three ways in which the classification systems described above may be used to help in the design and running of role-plays.

- To clarify objectives and intents.
- To ensure an integrated exercise.
- As a debugging aid.

Objectives

The act of deciding what type of role-play is to be used forces the tutor to think about his aims and objectives. If the function of the role-play is to develop specific skills then it will be counterproductive to use a style which concentrates on the emotional attitudes of the players. If a role-play is used in which the main description of the roles lies in the realm of functions, powers and relationships then the effects of individual knowledge, skills or experience may confuse the issue if they are allowed to intrude. In the same way, a role-play set in the past may be too distancing to enable students to appreciate its applicability to their current problems; it may be better to set it in the present or even the future.

The use of classifications to clarify objectives is a reiterative one: having set an initial set of objectives the tutor may decide on a particular way of running the role-play and this decision may suggest a slight change in direction in order to use the technique to the best advantage. This may in turn suggest another modification to the technique and so on until the best solution for the moment is found.

Integration

An important aspect of designing and using any teaching material or exercise is that of integrating all the elements together into a mutually supportive whole. In the case of role-play this means that the scenario, the roles and the background briefing must match the action in such things as the degree of detail, the atmosphere and so on. Furthermore, the way in which the debriefing is conducted must match the lines of the role-play and not be seen as a disjointed piece added to the end without thought. Once the type of role-play and its characteristics have been determined the tutor is in a better position to see how the separate elements fit together as a whole. The identification of the role-play type gives the tutor something which connects the beginning, middle and end of the exercise and ensures that there is no unexplained discontinuity between, for example, the outlined objectives of the role-play and the questions asked during the debriefing.

Debugging problems

Sometimes role-plays do not work. More frequently they work but not as well as their author or organizer expected. Experienced role-play users will recognize the phenomenon well. At such a time the tutor, probably exhausted by his efforts, will put the lack of complete success down to 'one of those things', 'the wrong time', 'the wrong atmosphere', the ineffectiveness of students or colleagues, or just the whims of fate. Perhaps some time afterwards he may want to take a more logical and systematic look at what may have gone wrong. The classification of different types of role-play is one way of putting some structure into the post-mortem.

There are a number of reasons why a role-play can go less successfully than expected. Very often it is a question of mismatch between the expectations of the tutor and students. A common way for this to occur is when tutors are working on one set of assumptions, but convey another by their actual instructions and techniques. Tutors may wish to give students the opportunity to see how they would behave at an interview, ie sensitize them to their own actions and speech, but structure the session with so much technical detail that they are searching to find their way within the simulation itself. Alternatively, tutors may want students to learn about the economic problems of an African tribe but they write the role-play so that the real conflict is between the role-players, instead of between them and nature (or government bureaucracy). By trying to identify the type of role-play they are using and checking to see whether plans and instructions correspond to this same type, tutors may progressively debug problems in the role-play.

One of the most common causes of failure in running role-plays is making them too complex. Role-plays should be kept as simple as possible for the job in hand. One should not try to accomplish too much in one go. Hence the ideal way of going about things is to identify which is the principal type of technique to use for a particular purpose and to concentrate on that. Consider the objectives of the session, the capabilities of the students, the resources available and the range of possible scenarios, then pick the simplest and clearest approach and stick with that. It is always possible to elaborate, indeed it is rather too easy; it is not so easy to simplify once the complex interactions have started to emerge.

TIP Keep it simple.

Choosing a role-play

A checklist for choosing a role-play or checking the suitability of an existing one is given in Figure 4.5.

Does the chosen type match the objectives of the exercise?
Can the students cope with the demands made on them?
Is the debriefing session structured in sympathy with the chosen type?
What would happen if one of the characteristics was deliberately changed?
Are the resources suitable for this type of role-play?
Will the role-play expose personal feelings too much?
Is there any way of simplifying the scenario?
Are roles all defined in a similar way?
Is role-play the best way of achieving the purpose?

Figure 4.5 Choosing a role-play

Each type of role-play described in this chapter represents a valid and effective use of the technique. The important thing for tutors is to be clear in their own minds as to which type they intend to use. If they use one type but employ techniques appropriate to another, there is a real danger of distancing students, frustrating them, or even damaging them. On the other hand, the use of the right style with the right type provides a sensitive and precise instrument of learning.

5 Preparing for role-play

Introducing role-play to participants

The way in which a role-play is planned will depend to some extent on its position in the general teaching curriculum. If it comes at the beginning of a course then you will need to explain how the whole course is to be structured and why you have chosen to use a role-play at the very beginning. If the session comes in the middle of the course, it will be necessary to review what the class has been doing, the point which they have reached, and the specific way in which the role-play will illuminate certain aspects of the subject. If the role-play is used to bring together what has been learnt in other lessons, it will probably fall naturally into place and require the minimum of explanation. In any case the amount of explanation needed will depend to a large degree on the age and type of student involved. In the school situation activities may be accepted without question; in industry they most certainly are not.

But unlike many situations where the student is happy to accept a logical explanation of what the next lesson is going to be, there are psychological difficulties to be overcome before role-play can be used with impunity. There are as many variations in this area as there are tutors and students. In some cases the tutor may tread boldly and fearlessly into the beginnings of a role-play without raising any anxieties or doubts in the minds of the students. They may volunteer with enthusiasm to play their parts in front of their peers and risk exposing themselves to real or imagined criticism before a semi-public audience. In other cases, however, the tutor may find that there are considerable barriers to be overcome before a group of middle-aged businessmen or callow self-conscious teenagers will enter wholeheartedly into the delights which are in store for them. Most tutors accept that the problem of entering into role-play for the first time needs to be taken seriously.

The term 'role-play' seems to be regarded with suspicion by most adults and not a few children. To announce cold-bloodedly that 'we are now going to have a role-play' can be the death blow to the very activity which the tutor was hoping to develop. The intimation that one is being asked to 'act' and the fear of being exposed in public are strong deterrents to all but the most extrovert. If it is the first time that the students have been involved in role-play, or if their previous experience was an unhappy one, then it is essential that the tutor takes time and care to approach the idea in a gentle and gradual manner.

There are two main ways of approaching role-play for the first time. The choice of which one to use will depend on the age group of the students and their motivation. The first way, most successful with adults and those who have a strong motivation towards the subject matter of the lesson, is to use the subject itself as a lead-in. The alternative, which is best used with children or with adults whose objectives are less clearly established, is to use a class of activities known as 'warm-up games'.

The graduated lead-in

The key to this approach is not to force a role-play on the students but to let it arise naturally as a result of exploring the problems that they are interested in. It is best illustrated by means of an example.

Let us suppose that a youth club leader or social worker wishes to explore some of the problems of authority and understanding between parents and their children. The group has got as far as agreeing that there can be areas of disagreement on how far the prerogative of a parent extends. The tutor questions the group:

'Can you give me an example of a situation where a parent is likely to want to exert authority?'
'Well, say on the question of returning home late after a party.' 'Yes, particularly if you're a girl.'
'What would the parent do?'
'Probably they'd meet you when you came in and tell you to go to bed and they'd discuss it in the morning.'

'So let's assume that both parents are having breakfast and their daughter comes in having arrived home late the night before. What do they say?'
'What time do you think you came home last night?'
'Who says that?'
'The father.'
'And what does the daughter reply?'
'You know what time it was, you met me in the hall.'
'And then what would the father say?'
'Don't be so cheeky.'
'What is the mother doing all this time?'
'Well I think that she is waiting to get a word in.'
'And what would she say?'
'I think she'd want to cool it down a bit.'
'What would she actually say?'
'Did you enjoy the party, anyway?'
'All right, so we've got an idea of what might happen to begin with. Let's try and see what happens from there. Now you suggested that the father might say "What time do you think you came home last night?" Let's put a table here for the breakfast, and you two parents sit having breakfast. You come in and start to get your breakfast and father – you say, "What time do you think you came home last night?", and you reply "You know what time it was, you met me in the hall". And we'll carry on from there.'

And so the role-play has begun, using the problem situation and initial words suggested by the group. Note that an imaginary activity such as having breakfast, or writing out a form helps to fill the initial silences and gives the role-players something physical to occupy themselves with.

In some cases it may be useful to begin much further back in the process. Starting with a general problem, you can gradually refine it down and separate out the interpersonal element which is the aspect you wish to deal with at that particular time. From there it should be possible to get an example and hence develop a role-play. The problem or difficulty should, whenever possible, be presented in situational rather than behavioural terms, ie what is happening rather than the behaviour that appears to be causing it. The two are not easily separated but if, initially, the tutor can put the emphasis on the general situation, the framework of constraints and the effects which a system is producing rather than individual behaviour, then students are more likely to approach the role-play with an open mind. You should also resist the temptation to pose the problem in such a way as to indicate your own solution, but should leave the outcome to the students as in the following example:

'Would anyone like to say what their biggest current problem is? Yes John, what's your current problem?'

'As far as I am concerned, it's the mistakes and extra work created by the computer invoicing system.'

'But I thought that computers speeded up the work?'

'Yes, but our computer department operates such a rigid system. For example the way they insist on all-numeric codes.'

'And mistakes? How can the computer make mistakes?'

'It's not really the computer itself I suppose, but the data isn't checked properly.'

'What does the head of the computer service section say?'

'Well, I suppose he's under pressure. But the system doesn't seem to be able to make the simplest correction without a mountain of paper work. And delays in getting out invoices cost us a lot of money.'

'What have you done about it?'

'I've complained of course – told him to buck his ideas up a bit.'

'Can anyone think of another way of approaching him?'

'I suppose one might have asked for his help and cooperation, explained the problems, and asked how one could help him with his.'

'That sounds reasonable David; how would you open the conversation?'

'I'd have said something like "Could we discuss the invoice problem and see what we can do to get round it."'

'All right, would you try that approach? Susan can be the computer services manager, and John can watch and give you a prompt about the details when you need it.'

Note that the tutor did not start by saying 'What changes should be made to the way the computer operators work?', or 'How could one ensure that the person who checks the invoice gives the job a higher priority and accepts non-numeric coding?' The students are left to identify the possible solutions and the way they might be implemented.

In this way the group can home in on a real problem which faces one of its members. The interest and challenge of such a problem will normally carry them through the first experience of role-play. Although for the sake of brevity the dialogue above has been made succinct, in practice the last stages of the discussion would probably lead to John taking aside the two role-players and briefing them in some detail about the problem. Alternatively he could take aside David, whilst other members of the group discuss the computer services manager's attitude with the student, Susan, who will role-play that part. One of the major advantages of this approach is that the tutor can encourage students to look at both sides and try to understand the problems faced by both participants.

There are many other ways of starting these simple, introductory role-plays. You can ask for an indication of a problem area – how to ask for a refund of money on faulty goods for example. You can then suggest the scenario -'Let's suppose that Jane is going into this shop with a transistor radio she bought yesterday. . . ' – and ask for the lead-in sentences from the group. Alternatively he may have a very simple example prepared with the first four or five lines of dialogue written:

> Arthur goes to get his money out to pay the conductor
> 'I'm sorry, but I seem to have left my money at home.'
> 'Well, I'm sorry, but you'll have to get off the bus.'
> 'But I've got to get home; it's too far to walk.'
> 'Then you'll have to pay, won't you?'

Using this method the tutor can either ask the role-players to say the lines and then continue, or ask them to discuss what should have been said, rewrite the first few lines, and then use them as before as a lead-in.

Other preparatory activities

There are of course other ways of getting the students to start thinking about the subject of the role-play. One method is to ask them to study a text and make notes on it. Or they may be asked to write a letter or memo which acts as the starting point from which the role-play can be developed. Another type of stimulus is pictorial. They may be shown diagrams, charts, graphs, pictures and be asked to discuss them. In particular one can use ambiguous pictures, similar to those used in the TAT (Thematic Apperception Test) in which people are asked to describe a situation and their answers are analysed to throw light on their personalities. In this case the pictures, which are deliberately vague and ambiguous, are used to provide a starting point for discussions and from there into role-play.

Case studies are a well-established means of teaching, particularly in the management field, but potentially in other areas as well. The teaching sequence usually goes from an analysis of the problem straight to a discussion of potential solutions. Role-play can be introduced between these two activities in order to give students greater insight into the problem. In this case the role-play can be suggested as a natural follow-on to the initial consideration of the case study and as a means of exploring it more deeply.

> **TIP** It is relatively easy to convert case studies into role-plays.

Questionnaires may also be used as a way of introducing the subjects for role-play. A questionnaire on how members of the group would react to or deal with a certain series of problems may be circulated and, after discussion, some of the respondents may be invited to act out their answers to see how they would work in practice. Students can also be questioned about the roles they have been asked to play. Such questioning can be a way of easing them into the role-play. One might ask, 'What does the shopkeeper feel?' or 'What will she start by doing?'

Finally the well-known buzz group technique can be used. In this approach the class is split up into pairs and every pair talks, argues or has a discussion at the same time. In applying this method to the start of role-play the tutor can get each pair to role-play a part of the problem, all working at the same time. The pairs may work on the same part or each pair could work on a different part. After ten minutes or so of this the group will be in a more informed and receptive mood to develop the main role-play. If role-playing in pairs is regarded as too threatening then getting the students to interview each other about the subject will be effective as a starter.

> **HINT** Interviewing can be a simple form of role-play.

Warm-up games

The previous section has approached role-play by eliciting the interest of the students in the subject or problems being explored. Sometimes they know too little about the subject to use this approach. It is sometimes more appropriate to concentrate on generating a relaxed atmosphere than to start with the subject of the lesson or session.

Warm-up exercises are an excellent way of breaking the ice and marking the change to a different type of classroom activity. They are quick, simple and require no knowledge on the part of the student. There are many exercises of this type, most of them handed down by word-of-mouth and demonstration from one tutor to another. There are now a number of books which contain collections of these games and the examples below are taken mainly from Davidson and Gordon (1978), Bond (1986) and Brandes (1979). Others are described in the various handbooks edited by Pfeiffer and Jones.

Talking down

Each person has a partner. A topic is given to them – such as: 'What happened to you this morning', 'Tell your favourite fairy story', 'Try and sell your partner an imaginary product or service'. They then talk simultaneously at each other and try to make the other person dry up. The period of interaction is limited to a very short time, say a minute or so.

A variation of this game is to play it in groups of three. A tries to talk to B or tell him a story. C's job is to sit near to A and B and use every means to try and stop B from listening to what A has to say – every means short of physical force that is. Again the time can be fairly short: two or three minutes will be adequate. If the players are not exhausted by then, the roles of A, B and C can be changed round.

Detective

Again people work in pairs. Without speaking, each person draws six items they have used in the last three months. Each in turn is the detective and guesses as much as they can about their partners. The partner remains silent until the detective has finished. Each person then introduces their partner to the whole group by saying what they have deduced about them.

Word-go-round

This exercise should be carried out in larger groups of four or more; it can be used with the whole class if desired. The idea is to tell a story but with each person contributing one word at a time in succession. As the story goes round the group there should be some pressure to keep up the speed. Beating a rhythm is an effective way of doing this. The topic for the story can be left completely open, or the tutor can suggest a subject such as 'Food', 'Travel', 'Hobbies' or 'Sport'. Either way it can be surprising to see the curious and bizarre directions in which the story line can go.

Advocates

A larger group of six or more is needed for this game. In the middle is the questioner who is trying to elicit information from the accused. But the accused, the person at whom the prosecutor is looking and talking, never speaks. It is always his advocate, the person sitting on his left, who answers for him. But the questioner can switch quickly from one person to another, in particular from a person to his advocate (the person on his left), and then his advocate has to answer. When anyone makes a mistake he becomes the new questioner in the middle.

These and many other games can be used to create the right atmosphere for using role-play. They must be used with caution, however. It is important not to be carried away by the fun and excitement generated by activities such as these and to remember that they are only there to act as an introduction; they are not an end in themselves. This has certain implications. The students must be clear, for example, that the purpose of these exercises is to help them acclimatize to the main part of the session; consequently the exercises should be kept to a relatively small proportion of the total time. It should also be recognized that they are for the most part fairly lightweight and deliberately so. Most students will soon tire of them and want to get on to something more substantial. In some cases this could be other exercises of a deeper and more complex nature; in others this will mean going on to the role-play itself.

Writing the scenario

After the participants have been introduced to the idea of using a role-play the next logical step is to familiarize them with its background. This brings us to the writing of the scenario – a task which involves the creation of a background, ways of describing it and the writing of briefs for each individual role-player.

Teaching objectives

In writing this scenario it is possible to begin with the overall picture and work towards detailed elements or vice versa. In practice, whichever approach is used the process tends to be a reiterative one where each stage is repeated several times. If one is going from the general to the particular, an overall scenario must be decided upon. Is it to be an interview in an office relating to an industrial dispute, a committee meeting dealing with a local authority decision, a family group, a point of sale transaction, etc? This will usually develop from a consideration of the general aims of the session. When considering these aims it is useful to begin by deciding whether the main purpose is to deal with:

- methods and skills;
- problems and principles;
- individual self-awareness and sensitivity.

This decision will then lead on naturally to a consideration of more detailed objectives.

Objectives may be expressed in a general way. For example, 'to give practice in the use of technical English', 'to give an understanding of the reasons behind the Williamson Committee and the 1919 Bill to rationalize the British electricity supply industry', 'to help students become aware of the implications of being Jewish', 'to enable officials to bargain more effectively', 'to improve interpersonal communication in project teams'. In some cases the objectives can be expressed far more exactly. In the case of language teaching, for example, one can make a list of what operations the student needs to perform, either in operational terms, ie to take notes, conduct an interview, make a request, describe, argue, advise, etc, or in linguistic terms, ie to use past tense, subjunctive, conditional phrases, develop vocabulary, etc.

The alternative way of starting on design is to identify the situation in terms of the characters involved and to work from that towards the general scenario. The dangers of this are that an over-emphasis on characters will develop and the generalized lessons to be drawn from problem situations will be lost. However, in practice it may be the problems posed by real characters known to the designer which stimulate the initial thoughts about the role-play. In this case one can try to extract general principles from the particular examples and approach the scenario with these in mind.

Constraints and considerations

Having determined the broad objectives or principles to be explored there are a number of details to be considered. First, there is the question of how the role-play is placed in relation to the rest of the course. Is it to be used as an introduction, to illustrate a particular problem, or as a summary of what has been learnt? Is it a central piece of learning, or marginal? This decision about its place and function will have an important influence on the structure and running of the role-play.

Second, the experience and background of the students need to be considered. In any teaching situation it is wise to start from where the student is, ie to use information, examples, ideas that are relevant and easily understood by the particular group of pupils or trainees in the class. The student's age, work experience, intelligence, social background, and – most important – expectations should be taken into account in making decisions about the background situation to be simulated, the problems presented and the characters involved in the role-play.

Where a specific organization or system is being examined one of the considerations at this stage is how close the scenario should be to the actual situation. Although it is useful to model role-plays on real situations there is an argument for keeping them slightly divorced from particular examples because:

- irrelevant facts may be introduced;
- defensive behaviour is encouraged if the chief actors can be identified;
- participants may want to duck out of responsibility and maintain that the faults lie outside the role-play situation.

Briefing

Having decided on the general scenario it is helpful to write a short draft introduction. This serves two purposes. It helps to clarify the designer's mind and it also acts as a reminder that the role-play must start with a form of introduction either verbal or written;

designers should ideally provide this as part of their design. This is an opportunity to decide on the method of briefing the players and in particular whether this should be done some time before the role-play takes place. Briefing will probably need to be in two stages: stage one is mainly concerned with filling in the broad background and can be written in the past tense, 'The department was established to co-ordinate the work', 'George has always wanted the club to buy its own premises'; stage two is concerned with the immediate problem and should be written in the present tense, 'There is a meeting arranged', 'The probation team is dealing with the case'.

Scenario

Where the subject is neutral the role-play designer may also want to make the role-play interesting and stimulating by building in certain elements of conflict (conflicting motives and emotions, perceptual differences, divergent goals, competition, scarce resources). It is these elements that usually contribute to the problem under review. When this is done the designer may find it useful to build in a potential resolution of the conflict as well.

The tutor may decide to place the action in an office, at a coffee bar, at a public meeting or in the street. The time may be the present, the past or the future. Clearly this will depend partly on the purpose of the role-play but if unfamiliar surroundings are to be simulated it is essential to close the gap between what the student may be expected to know already and what he needs to know in order to take part in the role-play. This will affect the briefing instructions.

Materials

The writing of the scenario provides an opportunity for the tutor to create an atmosphere by the choice of documents used. The background information may be presented in the form of a newspaper, a tape-recording, a prospectus, a set of official documents or some other medium.

> **TIP** Give the players information in a form that seems part of the role-play itself.

Depending on the purpose of the role-play and the resources available, the tutor may choose to make the materials more or less elaborate. On the whole it is detrimental to role-play if the players have to refer to documents during the action. In the case of the scenario, however, it may be possible to produce the information in such a way that it is not only legitimate but a necessary part of the role-play to use the documents for reference. This may add to the realism and at the same time avoid the need for players to memorize large quantities of data when it is needed in more sophisticated types of role-play.

HINT Remember that the aim is to provide role-players with just enough information to explore a specific problem without overloading them with unnecessary details or facts.

HINT If it is impossible to reduce the amount of information, it may be better to use a case study rather than a role-play.

Writing the role-briefs

The description of roles for the players themselves is of course central to the question of organizing role-plays. The structure of the role-play will be entirely determined by these roles and there are three types to decide upon.

- Key roles – These are the protagonists between whom information must be exchanged. They are the roles which effectively define the problem areas. It is important for the structure of the role-play that the players in these principal roles should feel able to influence the outcome of their encounters. If they are there only to feed external decisions into the role-play, this should be accomplished in some other way, otherwise the role-play ceases to be a genuine encounter of any substance.
- Subsidiary roles – These support the key roles. They may act as information givers, ie secretaries, clerks, officials, professionals; they may provide moral support, eg members of the family, teachers, advisers; they may act as adjudicators, eg chairmen, teachers, managers, parents, officials.
- Spare roles – in many cases the role-play may need to be used with

a variety of groups of different sizes and different abilities. Although some participants may be needed as observers, it is useful to have extra roles which can interest and occupy surplus participants. Unless these are thought out carefully beforehand, last minute additions can lead to situations where the extra role-player has little to do. It is better to devise roles which keep the player legitimately occupied. These are likely to be quasi-observational, eg minutes secretary, reporter, score keeper.

The characters in a role-play serve a number of purposes. The main characters, the protagonists, are the ones who provide both the central problems and an opportunity for role-players to exercise their skills. In many two-character role-plays they are the only characters who need to be introduced. In other cases, however, subsidiary characters may be used to provide information, present problems or control the action. In casting these roles the tutor may have to remember that students playing different roles will learn different things and also that it may be frustrating to play a person who has no control over the outcome of the simulation.

Fitting roles to role-players

It is unlikely that the sex, age, physical build, etc of the role-players will exactly match the image of the roles that you are developing. Decisions need to be made as to how to handle this. There are a number of ways round the situation.

- Build in neutral roles, ie 'Fletcher serves on the cold meat counter', 'You are Pat's grandparent.'
- Design the roles to fit the students. (This can be a dangerous practice because it reveals in public exactly what you think about the student.)
- Ignore the overt problem and use players irrespective of age and sex. Given a certain amount of assurance on the part of the tutor this can be one of the most successful approaches. It is essential, however, that the role-play designer makes his intentions very clear and anticipates any problems that may occur. One such problem is lack of background knowledge because the player is of the wrong age, sex or social class to have that knowledge. This can obviously be overcome in the design of individual briefs. Age and

sex differences are not likely to cause problems with adults who genuinely want to explore role-play. They may be more disruptive or inhibiting in the case of adolescents or children, although the difficulties are usually overestimated by the beginner.

If the problems of compatibility are sufficiently serious and are recognized at an early stage it should be possible to change the angle of view and re-design the role-play. It may be possible to look at a problem from the customer's point of view, the provider's point of view or the point of view of a complete outsider, depending on how the brief is written. For example, the relationship between midwife and expectant mother might also be explored through the eyes of the husband, a friend or another professional, as well as or instead of the original characters.

Role features

The writing of individual roles can best be done in two stages: the key features and the intended actions. As a start, for each role list the key features or resources available to the character:

- knowledge;
- skills;
- motivation and beliefs;
- constraints and pressures;
- power and authority.

When looking at the knowledge which characters might possess it is also useful to consider the sources of their knowledge, in other words the lines of communication between them and the other characters and between them and the world outside the role-play arena. This may in itself give the designer some ideas on how to structure the interplay of the exercise. It is also important to decide how much information is shared between roles and how much is special privileged information which is only available to the role-player in question.

HINT Include some questions on aspects that the character has in mind to explore.

Among the constraints and pressures to which the character is subject may be such things as age, sex, health, intelligence; likewise the sources of power and authority may be physical, organizational or social. The way in which these parameters are handled by you in designing the role-play will relate to the theories which you have about why people behave in particular ways, and the effects of such parameters on their behaviour. At all events you should endeavour to be consistent in your attitudes and put the same amount of detail with regard to these factors in each of the principal role-descriptions.

If a character holds particular attitudes or is in a particular emotional state then this should be derived as far as possible from the above features. The designer must avoid the temptation to write them in as part of the role itself. For example, it is bad practice to write 'You are prejudiced against black people. You are right wing in outlook and you feel very angry about your next door neighbour'. This is not looking at the situation from the role-player's point of view. Nobody likes to admit that they are prejudiced and one person's interpretation of right wing is not the same as another's. Similarly, being told that you are angry tends to encourage play-acting rather than an understanding of the problems of the role character. It would be better to say 'The black people living near to you seem to do very little work and yet they drive flashy cars. When you speak to them they don't give intelligent answers. Your next door neighbour is unreasonably noisy late at night and you have decided to take a firm line. You have made various attempts at getting the noise stopped but every time he gets away with it. Nobody seems to care about your problem'. This way of describing the role allows room for manoeuvre on the part of the player.

> **HINT** Write the role from the point of view of the role-player. After all, everyone thinks they themselves are rational, unprejudiced, nice people!

To put it another way, to write 'you think that the earth is flat' as part of the brief for a flat-earther is like saying 'you think that electricity makes the light come on when you operate the switch' to someone else. These are beliefs that accord with 'common sense' and can therefore be assumed as fact for the person who believes them. Otherwise one implies that it is only a belief and not 'really' so for the person concerned; this makes it impossible for the role-player to behave as the person they are playing would.

Intended actions

The first half of the role-description covers the above features, the second half covers:

- who should the characters meet?
- under what circumstances?
- to do what? What decisions must they make?
- for how long?

> **HINT** Think in terms of the basic questions – What, Where, Who, How, When, etc.

Make sure that the players are either told what their goals are or know that they have specifically been left to decide them for themselves. Tell them what they are going to do, where, with whom, for how long. Build these in as a natural part of the situation, eg 'You have been asked by Dibbins to discuss the tea-break problem. You are about to go into his office; you have another appointment in 20 minutes'. 'You have been asked to produce an assessment of the case before the end of the afternoon'.

> **HINT** For complex role-plays it is useful to produce a grid showing the roles and the actions or objectives the players will be aiming for. This enables the trainer to keep an eye on progress.

Names and terminology

The comments above assume that the tutor is writing the role-play himself but even if a ready-made one is used it is useful to go through these steps to ensure that the role-play fits its purposes and, if necessary, to modify the roles and role-descriptions to the course requirements. Names should be simple and not jokey. The student cannot be criticized for not taking the session seriously when saddled with a name such as 'Mr Gloom', 'Miss Pert', 'Mr Grabbit'. If the role-play involves real people such as Stalin, Thatcher, Nixon, De Gaulle, the players may try to imitate the person rather than be themselves in that role. A better solution is to simulate a similar but fictional country or state. If there are a large number of roles to handle, you will find it convenient to name the characters in such a way that they start with different letters of the alphabet – Arnold, Bill, Charles – or Attwood, Baker, Cripps – so that you can use letters for your own purposes in organizing the event: A meets B who is the boss of C ....

> **TIP** Use a telephone directory to provide neutral names.

It is best to write in the second person; this makes the impact more immediate, ensures that attitudes are internalized and avoids the he/she problem. One should also use the type of terminology which would be natural to that particular role, eg:

'You are the Health and Safety Officer for Boorlight Plating Ltd. You were originally a work study engineer but you have since received training in Health and Safety. The materials used for electroplating are highly toxic and section 3(v) of the Plating Premises and Chemicals (Health and Safety) Act 1992 lays down strict regulations for their storage and use. A recent DTI circular stresses the need for face masks in the plating shop.

Last week John Prince, one of the operators, complained of a bad headache and was sent home. He is a bit of a malingerer and a barrack room lawyer and you have had problems with him before.

The MD has asked you to see him. Also at the meeting is the Plating Shop Supervisor, Bill Evens. You have already spoken to him but he was not able to give you much information at the time. He is a friendly and helpful type.

You are taking with you the analysis of effluent, a record of stack temperatures and the results of air quality ppm tests. The MD starts by asking you how the Health and Safety records are looking..... '

Instructions

As indicated above it is best to avoid descriptions of emotional states such as 'you are angry because...' or 'you are worried because. . . '. It may, however, be necessary to indicate the degree to which the player should be willing to take risks or certain actions.

Whatever type of role-play is being used, in essence it is an exercise in which the player is playing himself but under certain constraints. It is out of these constraints that the role is developed and the role-player is being asked to behave as he would if he himself happened to be, shall we say, foreign or disabled or lacking in certain types of experience. A suitable instruction to the role-player might say 'Do not behave the way you feel the person in the position described in your role should behave. Just behave as you feel you want to within the constraints of the role itself.' It can be helpful though to give the player enough background to know how much he, in role, feels those constraints to be restrictive.

Briefings must be kept short – very short. Role-plays should be 'low-input – high output'. The longer the briefing the more like a lecture the session will turn into and this will destroy the major effect of the role-play. The total amount of detail will relate to some extent to the type of role-play being used. The learning of specific skills may demand a tightly structured brief; on the other hand the less structured the brief, the more opportunity is given for the players to learn about themselves.

TIP Use coloured paper or cards to distinguish between roles and make distribution easier. Fold the top so that only the title role shows for distribution.

Players should be asked to learn their roles; in some cases they may have a brief opportunity to practice their roles and then the written descriptions may be abandoned.

Roles do not always have to consist of written descriptions of course; there is always the possibility of using video, film, photographs, radio bulletins as models to follow, especially where behaviour modelling is the basic purpose of the exercise. One ingenious technique is to use letters that the role-play character has written and which may express their attitudes. Where role-briefs are written down players should not have to refer to role cards once play begins; the role-brief should specifically say 'Do not consult your role card once you have started the role-play'. Essential information should be presented in an alternative way, eg in the form of a reference document which might normally be available, via another role-player such as a secretary, or by some other mechanism like a newspaper; other information should be invented by the players as they go along.

Player invention

If briefings are to be kept short, the question remains of how the detail is to be filled in. What do role-players do when faced with a question on which they have not been briefed? The answer is simple: they invent and create whatever is necessary to fill out the part and keep the action going.

This of course raises the crucial question of what is legitimate invention and what is disruptive and likely to change the whole pattern of the exercise. This relates closely to the way in which the players expect to play their parts; it lies at the heart of a successful role-play. In essence the players must put themselves in a certain situation and then react to it as themselves but within the constraints and resources of the situation. The important point is that they are playing themselves, not trying to 'play act' and imitate the characteristics of another person except in so far as they are bound by the situation.

If, for example, someone is playing Admiral Nelson, there is no point in their having one eye covered by an eye patch, holding one arm in a sling or talking in the accent which they imagine him to have had if the main purpose of the simulation is to analyse the military decisions which he had to make in a particular battle. On the other hand, if the purpose of the role-play is to investigate the extent to which physical disabilities might affect a commander's influence at the conference table, these attributes might become extremely important.

Similarly, if the scenario called for Nelson to visit a village in order to urge the villagers to join the navy then the social distinctions of accent might play an important part. The point is that the situation should be allowed to dictate the constraints and opportunities, and the constraints and opportunities should shape the way in which the player performs.

HINT The most successful scenarios are those which excite interest and also contain a certain degree of uncertainty.

All the time the players must try to be themselves, but within the actual situation demanded by the scenario. In this way the simulation will become real to the participants and many of the problems caused by players being divorced from the action will disappear. This means that the main efforts of the creator of the role-play should be towards identifying the key factors in the situation – which is why writing role-plays and simulations can be such an effective way of learning about a subject!

Allocating roles

Roles may be allocated in a number of ways:

- randomly;
- allocating key characters and distributing the remainder randomly;
- assigning players to roles which fit them closely;
- deliberately choosing players with characteristics opposite to those of the role;
- letting the group discuss the allocation of roles amongst themselves;
- rotating roles between all the students.

The choice of method depends on the purpose of the role-play and the particular group with which the tutor is working. The following notes are intended as pointers rather than hard and fast rules.

If the objects of the exercise are to achieve maximum realism or to develop effective speaking then players should be cast to type, ie by playing roles near to their own real life position. Note that allocating children the same roles that they play in real life can be a mistake if those roles are unflattering; with adults it is easier for the tutor to judge what the effect might be. Otherwise, if the objectives are to give role-players an opportunity to experiment with their behaviour and become more sensitive to the attitudes and motives of others, it is better to cast against the player's own type. Ideally in this situation one should structure the roles to be played by extroverts in order to limit them; conversely one can leave the other roles, played by introverts, free of constraint.

In general it is easier to experiment with roles in a familiar scenario setting than in an unfamiliar one since the player's attention will be taken up in dealing with the background situation in the latter case, and they will not be able to give the necessary attention to the new aspect of the role.

TIP When picking out students for role-playing, it is advisable to wait at least 20 seconds after asking for volunteers before giving up. The next best choices are those people who maintain eye contact with the tutor.

If a discussion of the problem has been part of the initial warm-up procedure then the tutor can use those students who have expressed most interest during the warm-up discussion if a choice has to be made.

It is suggested at various points in this book that the tutor may wish to take part in the role-play for one reason or another. This clearly needs to be considered with care but if it proves necessary then one way to ensure the least confusion is for the tutor to take a part which is distinctly different in type to the general run of parts in the role-play. This removes the need to appear like everyone else and avoids some of the potential incompatibility.

Another slightly unusual aspect of role-allocation is the building of a number of 'assistant' roles into the role-play. These are suitable key positions which are filled by students who can be relied on to carry the role-play along. It is most suited to the 'public meeting' type of role-play used in the school situation but doubtless could be used elsewhere as a way of taking pressure off a harassed tutor.

Briefing the observers

Observers are useful in some role-plays, essential in some, and not needed in others. The most common situation where observers are needed is when the role-play is used to provide skills training and 'rehearsal' experience for the student. In some cases the tutor may act as observer, in others it may be more useful to appoint one or more of the class to help him. The observers themselves may be taking part, as actors, in the role-play in the characters of reporters or similar roles; they may be sitting or standing apart from the players, or they may be observing in another room through one-way screens or on video screens.

Some of the most useful material for role-plays emerges at the debriefing stage and it is essential therefore that careful attention is paid to the methods of observation and that observers are fully briefed. It may be that the original designer has a clear picture of what needs to be observed; the tutor may decide upon structure and observation, or the role-players themselves may be involved in deciding on the observations. Certainly the latter will ensure that the reports of the observers are more meaningful to the role-players since they have been commissioned, as it were, by the role-players themselves.

TIP   Reduce anxiety by involving participants in deciding what is to be observed.

In any event, whatever preparation for observation is made, the tutor should make sure that observations relate to both the content (what actually happened within the role-play) and the process (how, or why it happened).

The observation of role-play can be carried out at different levels. There is the task of noting physically observable acts including movements and speech; this requires a low level of inference. There is also the more sophisticated task of noting abstract qualities such as sincerity, aggression, support; this requires a much higher degree of inference and ideally needs trained and experienced observers if their conclusions are to be relied upon. Most tutors do not have the good fortune to have trained observers and must therefore try to brief their own; they should make allowance for this and not place undue weight on comments which are not observations of physical fact but inferences about attitudes and states of mind.

Observation schemes

There are many observation schemes which have been devised by psychologists for carrying out interaction analysis. In these schemes the observer notes instances of such activities as 'shows passive acceptance', 'shows tension', 'asks for opinion', 'asks for orientation, repetition, confirmation'. These observation sheets are developed from theoretical considerations and used for experimental work.

The type of observation which is used for role-play in education and training should be more problem-oriented and use broader categories. Much useful observation can be done by alerting the observers to key items of interest. Examples of the type of question that can be used are given in Figure 5. 1.

It is even better in many cases to use a more structured framework for observation. The general format of an observer grid is shown in Figure 5.2. It can be seen that there are a number of behaviour categories listed down the left-hand side with the names of roles across the top. Every time the behaviour occurs the observer puts a mark in the appropriate box. In the example Role B has exhibited Behavioural Category 4 seven times whilst Role C has not shown any signs of it at all.

There are various ways of approaching the task. It is possible, for example, to get individual observers to watch individual role-players and thus get more detail of, and empathy with, that player's actions. It is also possible for the observers to treat the whole group as one entity and monitor the general group behaviour or atmosphere every few minutes so as to get a picture of how behaviour varied over a period of time.

As far as the behavioural categories themselves are concerned, the tutor can either use a general purpose set or develop one for himself. Figure 5.3 gives an example of a practical set of observational categories which is well-tried and suitable for a variety of situations. Once the tutor is used to the idea of using these categories it is best to encourage the group members to construct their own. A good time to do this is during the warm-up period when students can be asked not only what problems they would like to work on but also what they would like the observers to take particular note of. This way they get feedback on precisely the points they want and it may be possible to re-run the role-play to see how much improvement there has been.

A natural problem which arises in connection with briefing the observers is what to do with the players whilst the briefing is going on. It may be possible to brief the observers separately by using a colleague, or to see them in a break before the session. If it has to be done during the session itself, however, then time can be saved by preparing observation forms and notes. The players themselves can be occupied by reading the scenario and their roles and possibly by taking part in some preliminary warm-up role-plays.

Who spoke the most/least?

When did people interrupt before others had finished?

What questions/arguments were never answered?

How did the general atmosphere change during the session?

What other solutions were overlooked?

Did speakers maintain eye contact?

Did you feel each person was listening?

Were people encouraged to air their views?

How much manipulation was going on?

Did joking help or hinder the communication?

What signs of frustration, boredom, enthusiasm, etc did you see?

Which members had high influence and which low?

Who kept the discussion on the rails? How?

Which actions helped the TASK (the problem being worked on)
and which helped the PROCESS (the way it was being tackled)?

How were silences interpreted?

Who talks/doesn't talk to whom?

How were decisions made?

Did the group structure their use of time?

Were any issues side-stepped?

Figure 5.1 Questions for observers

Roles / Behavioural categories	Role A	Role B	Role C	Role D
Category 1	11	111	卌	11
Category 2	卌 卌 111	1111	11	111
Category 3	11	卌	111	卌 卌
Category 4	111	卌 11		111
Category 5	11	111	1111	11
Category 6	卌	11	卌	11

Figure 5.2 Observer grid

Proposing Behaviour which puts forward a new concept, suggestion or course of action (and is actionable).

Building Behaviour which extends or develops a proposal which has been made by another person (and is actionable).

Supporting Behaviour which involves a conscious and direct declaration of support or agreement with another person or his concepts.

Disagreeing Behaviour which involves a conscious, direct and reasoned declaration or difference of opinion, or criticism of another person's concepts.

Defending/attacking Behaviour which attacks another person or defensively strengthens an individual's own position. Defending/attacking behaviours usually involve overt value judgements and often contain emotional overtones.

Blocking/difficulty stating Behaviour which places a difficulty or block in the path of a proposal or concept without offering any alternative proposal and without offering a reasoned statement of disagreement. Blocking/difficulty stating behaviour therefore tends to be rather bald, eg 'It won't work,' or 'We couldn't possibly accept that.'

Open Behaviour which exposes the individual to risk of ridicule or loss of status. This behaviour may be considered as the opposite of defending/attacking, including within this category admissions of mistakes or inadequacies, provided that these are made in a non-defensive manner.

Testing understanding Behaviour which seeks to establish whether or not an earlier contribution has been understood.

Summarizing Behaviour which summarizes, or otherwise restates in a compact form, the content of previous discussions or considerations.

Seeking information Behaviour which seeks facts, opinions or clarification from another individual or individuals.

Giving information Behaviour which offers facts, opinions or clarification to other individuals.

Shutting out Behaviour which excludes, or attempts to exclude, another group member (eg interrupting, talking over).

Bringing in Behaviour which is a direct and positive attempt to involve another group member.

Figure 5.3 Behavioural categories

Table reproduced from Rackham, N and Morgan, T (1977) *Behaviour Analysis in Training* McGraw Hill (UK) Ltd

Other preparations

Other preparations will depend on the way in which the role-play is being organized. In some cases tutors like to use a number of 'props', in others the additional material is kept to a minimum. It really depends on the purpose of the role-play, the type of student, and the personal style of the tutor. A few props may help to create the right atmosphere – too many will create the impression of a theatrical performance. In some cases additional materials are needed as an integral part of the role-play. If a person is required to write something down, carry something, inspect something, then it may be necessary to provide the real materials. If role-reversal is going to be used to give students an understanding of the problems of the opposite sex, for example, it may be useful to have handbags for male role-players to carry should the tutor feel that always having to carry something and remember to pick it up has a subconscious effect on behaviour. Likewise, sitting in a large executive tilting chair has a marked effect on people's attitudes and there are many similar examples.

It does not always have to be taken to the extreme, however. It is perfectly acceptable to represent a telephone conversation by having two people on either side of a screen, or to represent a machine by a box or table. As with all simulations it is important to identify the essence of the prop and to provide just that and no more. The essence may be the inability to see the other speaker, the weight of what is being carried, or the bulk of an object on the floor.

There are also practical accessories such as name plates or badges. If these are made large and legible, they avoid the unnecessary hiccup that occurs when one of the role-players forgets the name or role of another. One unusual but effective prop which tutors may find useful, particularly if they are dealing with an excited group of children, is a symbol to indicate that role-play is in progress or has stopped. The idea is similar to the use of a mace on ceremonial occasions. When the bell, or lump of stone or book is on the table then everyone is in role; when the symbolic item is removed the role-play is suspended.

Another aspect of preparation is timetabling. Most role-play activities can be broadly divided into the preliminary introduction and briefing, the role-play itself, and the post-play discussion or debriefing. Whilst it is desirable that these activities should run into one another continuously, it is often not practicable to do so. At the very least, however, the break points must be arranged to coincide with the natural breaks in the activity. Timetabling may also be needed to avoid the noise of a particularly boisterous session from disturbing other teachers or trainers who are trying to do their job in the adjacent room in a more conventional fashion!

As with any other activity, if the preparation has been done thoroughly and efficiently, the actual running of the role-play should not present many difficulties. The room(s) should be set out in the right way, paperwork arranged in easily accessible form, the players and observers properly briefed. Before going on to the running, however, there is an intangible hazard that can creep into the proceedings and linger there, teaching the wrong lessons. This is the hidden agenda, and we deal with it in the next chapter before looking at the actual running of the role-play.

6 *The hidden agenda*

An introductory probe

Let me try an experiment with you. Imagine a court room. The case before the judge is that of a cook who is married to an electrical engineer. Whilst the engineer has been working overseas on an important contract, the cook (who works in a local school) has had to call in a plumber because of a fault in the central heating system at home. Whilst the plumber was at work in the empty house, a friend of the cook's, an attractive 40-year-old nurse, came to call. The plumber made advances to the nurse and in the course of a slight scuffle the plumber fell on a valve which was being repaired and a valuable Chinese carpet was damaged by water.

The police witness who was called to the scene states that no one was injured and that the only other witness was a small child playing with a doll's house in the adjoining room. The prosecuting counsel, a stern-looking figure in wig and gown, rises to cross-examine the plumber. The court shorthand-typist prepares to take notes. The smartly dressed social worker waits to be called as an expert witness.

As the prosecuting counsel rises to her feet, she asks the plumber what time she arrived at the house. This is clearly intended to be used later when the nurse will be asked his version of the story. The judge listens carefully to the evidence, all her attention on the answers of the plumber ... Have I said enough? Are you confused?

Supposing I'd asked you at the end of the second paragraph for a description of the cook? What sort of a picture would you have had in your mind? Would it surprise you if I told you that he is a small thin man of Chinese descent and that his wife is a famous electrical engineer? What sort of clothes do you think the social worker was wearing? A smartly dressed social worker? Well? Not only that, but what about the police witness, and the judge, and the short-hand-typist? Most people will have had a preconceived idea of what sex these characters 'should' be. You no doubt will have kept a completely open mind ... oh yes, what about the sex of the small child?

Perhaps by now you will also have noticed that my style of writing has suddenly changed. Now I'm writing in the first person; now we see each other eye ball to eye ball so to speak. At the same time the words and phrases have become less formal. I'll explain why I have chosen to do this in a moment, but for the time being see if you have conjured up a picture of me. What is your picture of an author named 'Morry van Ments'? What is your picture of 'an author'? Am I a rotund Dutchman puffing on a pipe and tapping his clogs on the stone hearth? Or a lean and hungry looking academic with a serious face and an enormous family being kept quiet in the background? Or am I a dizzy blonde teetering around in a mini-skirt and high heels? It doesn't matter? Doesn't it? Are you sure that your reception of this book wouldn't be coloured just a little?

The problem is of course that personal characteristics can get in the way of some types of communication just as they can enhance others. Although for a fuller appreciation of some books it may be helpful to know a lot about the author's shape, size and colour, it can be distracting and irrelevant in other cases. Thus the impersonal style of third person writing has developed which avoids giving readers a needless attitude towards the book's author, so preventing them from concentrating on the subject matter. For this reason I have lapsed into time-honoured neutrality for the purposes of writing this book. It is not so easy to be neutral in a role-play, however, even when one wants to be; role-plays use real people playing real roles and it is much more difficult to dissociate personal characteristics from the role whether they be in the flesh or in the imagination.

Stereotypes in advertising

It is by now conventional wisdom that modern advertisements play on unconscious associations in the reader. Cigarette posters show cool mountain streams, woodlands and open air scenes to conjure up feelings of health, cleanliness and freshness instead of the reality of a smoke-filled atmosphere, catarrh and coughing. Advertisements for various forms of alcohol portray people having witty and friendly conversations in sophisticated surroundings, not by any means the way in which the bulk of alcohol is consumed. The marketing of food products and household cleaners is done by associating them with a loving family whose love seems to depend on food and cleanliness, whilst the subconscious associations between the choice of a car and sexual virility have been documented with delight by social psychologists.

These associations have been pointed out so often that one suspects that a certain amount of customer resistance has built up to the more obvious uses of association. There is however, another layer of subconscious which is being tapped, one which does not directly relate to the product being sold, but which underlies most of the fantasy world of advertisements.

Most of the characters in this dream world are white, middle class, happily married couples with children. They maintain a higher standard of living than the income associated with their jobs would normally support. Their behaviour reinforces the standard role stereotypes, eg the men bring in the money, wash cars, mow the lawn and read newspapers; the women do the washing, cook and talk obsessively about cleaning, babies and losing weight. The children are either full of energy and seen running up and jumping down stairs or miserable because they have colds. Nearly everyone is healthy and either young or at least a young-looking middle-aged person. Those non-white characters who appear are either not married or married to a person of their own colour.

Many of these stereotypes appear in films, books and plays. The danger of their appearance in advertisements is precisely because the advertisement is seen to relate to the 'real' world since it is selling real products. Anyone can buy a tin of X or drink Y and thereby become loved, admired, or successful. The tin is real, so why shouldn't the consequences be?

The stereotype in role-play

There are a number of reasons why the use of the stereotype in role-play is particularly important. In the first place role-play, as we have already seen, is a very powerful technique for shaping people's behaviour and attitudes. We have assumed up to this point that what is learnt is to some extent planned for and controlled by the tutor. But the student is likely to acquire attitudes which are moulded by any aspect of the role-play, whether intended or not. The visible agenda is what the teacher and student expect to be learnt, the hidden agenda is the 'space between the words', what is assumed and not overtly intended.

The problem is that the tutors, being human like everyone else, are bound to draw upon their own experiences and attitudes when writing the role-play material. Unfortunately what is learnt in a role-play is not only what is overtly described and planned for, but also the totality of the experience which the player goes through. This experience is bound to mirror to some extent the assumptions of the tutor.

Let us take a concrete example. In a role-play used for training bus conductors there were a series of incidents involving a secretary, a storekeeper and a bus passenger. The role of the storekeeper was allocated to a male, and that of the passenger (who was absent-minded, ineffectual and created a disturbance through losing an umbrella) to a female. As an isolated instance this allocation of roles would not matter but it is symptomatic of the way in which assumptions about people and their roles can be built into the role-play without the assumptions being made explicit. It would have been perfectly possible for the storekeeper to have been a woman and for the absentminded and scatterbrained passenger to have been a man. There is an increasing amount of concern being shown about the way in which sexism and prejudices of various sorts, including class and racial prejudice, can be exacerbated by the way in which roles are written and allocated. The fact that in most cases these attitudes are not overtly discussed means that they are more insidious and less easy for the student to resist.

Much of the structure of a role-play is designed to explore roles. As the name implies it is an activity which uses the concept of role as fundamental material. The purpose of the enactment is to see what happens when students in different roles are brought into confrontation either with each other or with the circumstances which constrain them. It should not surprise us therefore, if their perception of the roles which they and their peers are playing has a considerable effect on their own behaviour during the role-play. This behaviour will in itself affect the responses of the other players.

! WARNING !

Watch out for stereotyped behaviour generating self-fulfilling responses.

If, for example, a student is playing the part of a police officer he may adopt a crisp, brusque way of speaking and ask questions rather than give advice or information. The person playing opposite him may react to this by withholding information, going on the defensive, becoming less cooperative. The police officer will naturally have to exert more authority to get the information he requires. Thus the players' mutual expectations feed on each other until they begin to enact stereotypes of boss/shop steward, parent/child, teacher/pupil, or husband/wife, etc.

Since the student in a role-play learns from the consequences of role interactions, the learning will be based on the stereotyping and will therefore reinforce prejudices and preconceptions. Some role-play situations are designed to create empathy with the characters whose roles are interpreted. If, therefore, role-players find themselves playing characters whose surroundings encourage a certain attitude then this is the attitude that they will empathize with whether or not it was intended by the writer of the simulation. If, for example, students as characters in the role-play always find themselves dealing with immigrant workers or women whose roles dictate that they are low achievers, then the result will be a reinforcement of assumptions about these groups. Worse still is the situation where the character being played is put under pressure by others who may represent police officers, head teachers, managers, etc. The empathy which develops between the player and the role-character will leave a lasting impression of these authority figures which may not tally with their real behaviour.

Even these defects might be acceptable if it were not for the fact that role-plays use such a wide range of roles and that it is very easy to allow unconscious assumptions to creep into the role-briefings and general descriptions. Whether one likes it or not, the world picture given to the student is a fairly accurate reflection of the tutor's own ideas. It is the covert nature of this image and the extensive range of its subject matter which makes it so important.

The reinforcement of prejudice and social conventions, whether desirable or not, is part of the danger to beware of in the hidden curriculum and before considering how we may avoid these dangers it is necessary to explore this concept a little more.

The hidden curriculum

In her paper on the hidden curriculum Glandon (1978) points out that there are at least three areas in which unintentional learning may take place when using simulations: first, in the reinforcement of the authority and power of the teacher (whilst overtly appearing to be using a more democratic and egalitarian method of teaching); second, the embedding of common attitudes towards role behaviour in an apparently open set of role-descriptions; third, the rewarding and reinforcing of behaviour which 'plays the system' rather than behaviour which is socially desirable. Let us have a look at each of these areas in turn as they relate to role-plays.

Authority

Numerous attempts have been made in recent years to break down the barrier between teacher and taught, between therapist and client. The argument for doing this is that the purpose of education, and also that of therapy, is to make the subjects more self-reliant and able to carry on the process independently because they have learnt how to use the resources available to them; this includes regarding themselves as a resource.

The extreme manifestation of this attitude is the T-group, where the leader appears to abrogate all responsibility for the way in which the session is conducted and what the participants do. Other groups, such as encounter and gestalt groups (see Chapter 9) have leaders or facilitators but these facilitators still insist that the group members 'take responsibility' for what they do and what happens.

The organizers of a simulation or role-play also attempt to disclaim their normal role of authority. They withdraw from the action and state that they are not the expert or judge. Learning is supposed to flow from within the student and the student is supposed to be in control.

In practice this ideal cannot be attained. There is nothing wrong with this. The problem is that many tutors using role-play are oblivious to the fact that they necessarily have a controlling influence. The writer of the role-play knows the constraints which have been built in, knows how long he intends to let the exercise run, knows what the aims of the session are, and knows what is likely to happen, what may go wrong, what are the good and bad ways of acting in that particular situation.

Tutors must know the rules of the game and how far they are prepared to allow them to be stretched. They must keep an eye on the realities of the outside world and ensure that the role-play does not interfere with other people's activities. In the debriefing they know what they want to bring out, what important lessons are to be learnt.

The point is that tutors are keepers of knowledge, certainly as far as running a role-play is concerned. They have done it before, or at least have seen one run, or read about it. They know how the roles are written and distributed and what the objectives of the session are. The tutor's interpretation of events is likely to be the one which is taken as 'correct', and even when things do not go according to plan, the tutor can always explain what was 'supposed' to happen.

The result of all this is unimportant provided that the student is told that the tutor is in ultimate control and accepts the basic reality of that situation. The alternative is to put all the cards on the table and encourage the students to participate in the design and running of the role-play. This is possible, but demands greater expertise and flexibility on the part of the tutor. The benefit is that the conduct of the exercise lies closer to the concept of a student-centred activity and it is worth considering whether the extra effort might not be worth it.

HINT Build student participation into the design of the role-play in order to break down teacher/student barriers.

If the tutor wants to try greater student participation then a suitable procedure would be to start by explaining the point at which the class has arrived in the subject and why he feels it is a suitable point at which to introduce a role-play. This is very similar to the procedure discussed in Chapter 5. The class can then discuss the way they want to set up the role-play. During this the tutor explains the constraints, problems, etc. As suggested earlier, the observations to be carried out can be agreed with the players before the role-play; this

automatically determines the essence of the debriefing. If it is necessary to intervene during the enactment, the tutor can refer back to
what was openly decided by the class at the beginning.

By using this type of approach the tutor can make the class see
where authority derives from and avoid the situation where the student feels cheated by being led to expect a different student/tutor
relationship from what he actually experiences.

Role bias

This is the most insidious of the three areas of influence. In most
scenarios women appear as secretaries or housewives and men fill
all the roles which are potent, that is to say where they can directly
influence decisions which are being made. Blacks rarely appear, nor
do the disabled or adopted children, divorcees, the elderly or one-
parent families.

Where distinctive social roles appear such as the police officer,
social worker, landlord, trade unionist or politician, their roles are
written in such a way as to conform to the prevailing ideas on how
such people behave.

These generalizations may be broadly true in a statistical sense.
It may well be that most women are secretaries or housewives; your
chances of meeting a soft-spoken police officer or decisive social
worker may well be less than average. The point is that role-plays
often do not allow for there to be any chance at all of a woman manager, a non-militant trade unionist, a philanthropic capitalist.

There is a case for arguing that the out of the ordinary should at
least be represented as great a proportion of the time as it occurs in
real life. Moreover, because role-play is supposed to give people an
opportunity to try out their skills in a safe environment, there is a
strong argument for introducing the problem of dealing with a person who stutters, or one whose cultural background is different, or
a person whom one would not normally have the opportunity to
meet in that situation.

An even more pressing argument is that all those engaged in education and training are by choice of profession engaged in shaping
the attitudes and beliefs of their students. This arises unavoidably
from the way in which students perceive their teacher or trainer, and
model their behaviour on those to whom they look for instruction. Therefore, it behoves tutors to shape attitudes and behaviours
in the way they feel students should be moving rather than to allow

undesirable and rigid biases to go unchallenged.

However hard they try to avoid sex stereotyping, tutors are bound to find that there are many occasions when it is necessary to use the conventional sex roles or perhaps conventional age or nationality roles. Unless the main purpose of the role-play is to highlight these assumptions it may be too distracting to cast the role of a secretary as a boy, the managing director as a teenager, or a West Indian as the local lord of the manor. This is not to say that the secretary (assumed to be a woman) could not be played by a boy, the managing director played by a teenager or the English aristocrat by a West Indian; it is amongst the normal possibilities of role-play. What would be distracting would be to write into the actual role-descriptions the fact that the secretary was male, etc, because this would draw undue attention to that particular characteristic and might be undesirable unless the focus of the role-play was especially on those aspects.

What then can be done in cases where the tutor wishes to use stereotypes for convenience, but is conscious of a responsibility not to reinforce them? The answer is to deal with the problem in the debriefing phase. This can be done at two levels. In the first place the tutor can draw attention to the problems of stereotyping and ask the group to discuss the way in which assumptions were made in the describing and casting of roles. You should ask questions such as:

- were males and females given different roles?
- how far would the role-descriptions be interchangeable?
- did the functions of the role-players necessitate particular abilities?
- what assumptions were made about those abilities and why?
- why do we think that way? Could it be different?

At the second level the tutor may be able to draw lessons from the behaviour and attitudes of the group during the debriefing session itself. Attention can be drawn to the question of who does the most talking or acts as leader, provides useful analyses or information. Then one may question the extent to which the group itself is conforming to stereotype, and why or why not. The significant thing is to ensure that the subject is brought into open discussion where prejudices and myths may be exposed and positive suggestions made for overcoming them.

Before leaving the subject of role bias it would be fitting to justify again the author's decision to use the masculine pronoun through-out this book rather than 'his or her' or 'he or she'. In this revised edition a number of amendments have been made to make the text more neutral. This has highlighted two things: in the first place, that it is always possible to improve on one's first, and indeed second attempt; but secondly, it became clear that making the text neutral sometimes had the effect of making it bland and cumbersome. There are times when the direct use of a pronoun gives the argument a clarity, force and direct application which cannot be achieved in any other way, and the word 'his' by longstanding grammatical convention no longer has the force of an exclusively masculine word. The author feels, however, that by thus exposing his less than perfect solution he has at least drawn attention to the possible unconscious effects of his personal style of writing and hence kept his integrity within the context of this chapter.

Beating the system

Whatever the aims of the tutor, the motivations of the students will be closely bound up with success or failure within the structure of the role-play itself. They will judge themselves on such criteria as whether they achieved the result which was asked for and within the time limits set. They may ask themselves if they managed to get what they wanted regardless of whether the other students achieved their goals.

Sometimes the tutor's attention may be to teach the need for speed or assertiveness or individuality. Often, however, these will be merely the unlooked-for results of the way in which the role-play was structured in the first place. It is usually easier to give players individual goals than to cope with the complexity of group and individual goals in combination. Similarly it is common to put time limits on the role-play for obvious practical reasons. The tutor may feel that pressure must be put on the players in order to get the best from the role-play and this pressure materializes in the shape of constraints of action and time or the setting of goals that are difficult to achieve.

Since any role-play only takes a slice of life and must operate within an assumed set of boundary rules, there tend to be opportunities for the players to boost their 'score' by 'playing the system'. A player may neglect to spend time doing something which in reality he would do, take greater risks than he would normally, or take unpopular steps secure in the knowledge that he will not be around to have to live with their consequences. Conversely, he may decide to cooperate or give way for the sake of getting to the end of the enactment, or to get on to another, more exciting part of it.

HINT Structure the role-play to reward desirable rather than undesirable behaviour.

At the end of play the student will have been more or less successful in achieving his goals. These goals may not be the ones intended by the tutor; even more important, the way the student has learnt to reach his goals may not be the way the tutor intended. Speed may have been rewarded at the expense of accuracy, or decisiveness at the expense of cooperation. It is easier to set time limits than to check on the accuracy or validity of results, especially since the results may not be available until the end of the session. Decisions are easier to assess than abstract notions such as improved cooperation.

The solution in these cases lies at the beginning of the process rather than the end. Scenarios and briefs must be carefully thought out so that the aims and objectives of the role-players are clear. There must be initial understanding of what is considered reasonable behaviour and what would be regarded as unfair or unjustifiable. Even when these precautions are taken, however, it may be necessary to bring up the question of the desirability of some of the behaviour in the role-play. One technique, used more commonly in competitive games, is to shorten or lengthen the role-play without warning. This may reveal the way in which role-players are resting their behaviour on an expectation that life in the role-play will suddenly cease at a predetermined time. It forces artificial strategies out into the open. This is touched on further in Chapter 7 when discussing the role of the tutor.

A more difficult issue to deal with is the natural advantage bestowed upon the fluent and articulate student. Although there are some aspects of role-play that appeal to less educated and articulate students, as mentioned in Chapter 2, the fact remains that a lot of role-play depends on talking rather than physical activity. This puts a premium on verbal skills which is acceptable for some types of instruction such as salesmanship, teaching or interviewing but not necessarily in all cases. The tutor must use his own ingenuity in writing and allocating roles if he wants the non-verbal side of communication to be stressed. A fantasy world using a special language, or incorporating a deaf and dumb character are possible, although extreme, solutions. Another way is to stress the importance of non-verbal behaviour at the debriefing stage.

Summary

The ultimate protection against the unwanted learning which has been described in this chapter is the tutor's own awareness of the inherent dangers. Figure 6.1 gives a checklist which should be useful in this context.

---

1. Do not write in stereotypes. Keep to functions, powers and constraints.
2. Use deliberate non-conventional writing.
3. Cross-cast roles.
4. Use role-rotation.
5. Use debriefing session to question assumptions.
6. Invite students to challenge.
7. Ensure that reward systems encourage correct behaviour.

Figure 6.1 Avoiding unwanted learning

Having prepared the role-play material, the tutor is now in a position to set the wheels in motion, to let action commence.

7 Running the role-play session

By this stage tutors will have decided on objectives and how the session will fit into the curriculum. They will also have looked at constraints and factors affecting their choice. Lastly they will have written or obtained the materials for running the role-play. We have arrived at the block marked 'Run session' in Figure 7.1.

The basic techniques

Fish-bowl

There are many ways of organizing a role-play depending on its purpose and the type of student involved. We will look first at the two most straightforward and common methods and leave the more esoteric ways until later in the chapter. The first two are often known as the 'fish-bowl' and the 'multiple' approaches.

The fish-bowl technique is the one which most people will have had experience of if they have had any experience of role-play at all, and it is therefore the one they think of when they decide to use role-play. The principal players meet each other in the centre of the room and are observed by the other members of the class who sit in a rough circle around them. Subsidiary characters, where there are any, enter from the periphery of the 'stage' and return there when their part is done. There are of course variations on this: the whole class may be taking part and there will in that case be no observers;

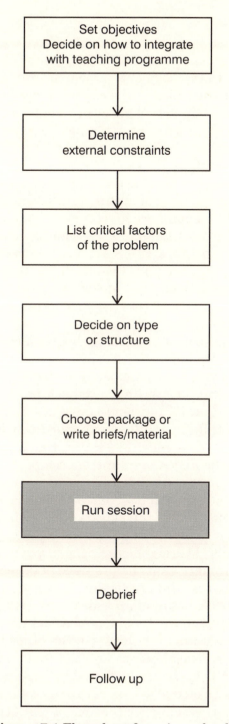

Figure 7.1 Flow chart for using role-play

the physical setting for the role-play may preclude the particular setting out as a fish-bowl, as for example where a public meeting is staged and the principal actors sit in the front of the room with the general audience in the body of the room; or the dimensions of the room may confine the action to one end with the observers sitting at the other. Whatever the actual physical layout, the term 'fish-bowl' denotes the idea of one group portraying the action whilst another group observes.

The fish-bowl technique has some fairly clear-cut advantages and disadvantages. It is in many ways the 'natural' format if one is considering role-play as a form of drama. It differentiates between the protagonists and the audience or observers and also allows those who for one reason or another do not want to take part to detach themselves from the action. It is also a very convenient form where detailed observation is required since all the observers can get a good view of what is going on. Moreover, since the whole group shares the same experience, they are in a better position to analyse it jointly.

But this emphasis on the similarity between role-play and theatre can be counterproductive. As we have seen, role-play is not play-acting and should give the participants the feeling of real life action and decision-making. The setting of the fish-bowl stresses the artificiality of the situation and lends credence to those who judge role-play to be nothing more than an opportunity for the extrovert and amateur theatrical buff. Moreover, the whole arrangement puts a strain on the players and introduces pressures which arise from outside the enacted situation. This can particularly be the case where the group is larger than eight to 12 people. These pressures can distort the reactions of the players who from time to time will be conscious of the presence of an audience.

One should not overemphasize this aspect; people running role-plays often remark that the presence of observers is soon forgotten by the players who are having to concentrate under their own pressures. The amount of information that the players have to handle and the demands on them to make decisions are usually sufficient to keep them fully occupied. On the other hand, a break in concentration at a crucial point may lead to an outcome which in retrospect is seen to have been affected by the presence of observers. Those who are asked to take part in a role-play for the first time are usually nervous of doing so; the idea of 'performing' in front of an audience is anathema to them even though they may have been assured by the tutor that they will not notice those surrounding them. Finally, the effect of using the fish-bowl technique is to restrict the enactment of each role to one person thus denying others the opportunity of trying out how it feels; it also depends of course on the effectiveness of those chosen to perform the role-play.

Multiple

An alternative approach is the 'multiple' technique. In this the class is split up into a number of small groups of two or three students and each group enacts the role-play at the same time. In other words a number of identical role-plays take place in parallel. The small groups may consist of just the players, or may also include observers. The classic way of using this method is where the class wants to explore the interaction between two people in either formal or informal interviews. There may, therefore, be two players and one observer in each group.

With this technique the players feel less embarrassed and exposed and can come to terms with an interaction which is only seen by one or possibly two of their colleagues. It also enables a number of different interpretations to be tried out simultaneously and can therefore take up less time. After everyone's role-play has finished the class can meet together to exchange experiences and draw on the range of things that took place.

On the other hand no two people will have observed the same role-play and it is difficult to check on exactly what happened and why. Since the objective of a number of role-plays is to demonstrate the communication problems thrown up by differences in interpretation and perception this can be a major disadvantage of the multiple method. It is compounded by the fact that the tutor will be unable to observe more than one interaction at a time and is likely to miss some of the crucial incidents that took place – the use of well-trained observers can therefore be invaluable. A further practical problem is that one group may finish ahead of the others and be left waiting.

These then are the two main, simple ways of setting out the role-play. Other variations arise from the need to deal with running problems, or in order to develop the basic role-play further. We will look at these after we have covered the basic running itself.

Starting the role-play

The start of the actual role-play is usually fairly straightforward. It may be that the design of the warm-up is such that it leads smoothly into the role-play without a break. In other cases the class has been briefed in a previous session and can be left to organize its own starting procedure as it enters the room for the beginning of the session. In the majority of conventional role-plays it will be necessary for the tutor to give some sort of starting signal. Although this may appear to be a trivial detail it is important in that this is the time when the boundaries of the role-play must be clearly defined in everyone's mind. The participants should be clear as to when they are 'in' the role-play and when the rules governing it apply.

The type of lead-in will vary with the tutor and the particular scene to be played. In some cases it is appropriate to provide a situational start; the tutor may say 'I'd like you to take over as chairman and start the meeting', or 'The interview begins with John coming through the door', or 'You are sitting eating breakfast when Sheila enters from upstairs'.

A less usual way of starting a role-play, but one which may be of use where there already exists a good rapport between the tutor and students is for the tutor to switch into a suitable role and to start the role-play from within it. This can give the role-play a flying start provided the tutor has energy and a little charisma. It is certainly well worth considering. For example: 'Well I'm glad to see that so many of you have turned up for the meeting about the proposed by-pass, and I'll introduce your chairman to you so that you can get straight on with the business of the meeting. Now I'm sure that many of you will know Councillor James but for those of you who are new to the district. . . ', or 'I've arranged the interview room for you here Mr Taylor. I'll fetch the first candidate along when you're ready. We normally break at 10.30 for coffee. Is there anything else that you'd like me to tell you ...?'

Another way of beginning is to provide part of a script. This may consist of a fairly lengthy lead-in dialogue, or at the other extreme just a sentence or part of one: 'You're late again', 'Please tell me what the problem is', 'I want to ask you about. . . '. In most cases the players will have been told what these opening statements are; in some cases, however, the tutor will want to give them practice in dealing with unexpected situations and will leave one or more of the players in the dark, and it is worth making a comment at this point about the withholding of information.

Giving and withholding information

Clearly the tutor will have an idea of what he hopes to achieve and will want to make decisions about the amount of information given to the players. Feeding information through in manageable doses is a useful technique for preventing too much of an overload on the student; deliberately withholding information is another matter and needs to be treated with caution. The tutor should always be aware of the temptation to 'play games' with the group and see 'what happens if . . . '. It is vital to the success of the role-play that it is taken seriously by the participants and that they regard the outcome as reasonable under the particular circumstances. If they do not then nothing will be learnt because they will regard the situation as an artificial one, completely controlled and manipulated by the tutor and therefore not a representation of reality.

Information which is deliberately withheld should fit into the natural bounds of the role-play. In a number of interview situations there will be information that one of the participants does not know – indeed part of the purpose of the interview will be to extract that information. If a cross-cultural simulation is being used where members of two cultures interact with one another then it will be part of the simulation to make sure that they are ignorant of each other's customs.

! WARNING !

Only withhold information that would be withheld in real life.

A more difficult situation is one where a role-player is presumed ignorant of something which lies within his own background. If a family scene is being played out, for example, it may be that the father does not realize that his son has been sacked from his job, whereas the mother does know. These pieces of information and the way in which they are given or withheld can alter the whole running of a role-play and must be used with care. Often the reason for withholding information at the beginning of the action is in order to feed it in at a later time. This will be dealt with a little further on in this chapter.

Inventing new information

At this point the enactment has begun: the observers are in place and the players have begun speaking. If the preparation has been done well the role-play should run smoothly. There are always unforeseen incidents, however, and it is as well to be prepared for them. One thing which can produce problems for the inexperienced is the question of how much the role-players should invent as they go along. The need to invent will always be present in the well-written role-play. It indicates that the writer has allowed sufficient leeway for the players to inject their own thoughts and ideas into the action, otherwise one is forcing the players to work within such a tight script that it might just as well be a play.

Moreover, it is impossible to predict exactly what information the players are going to need, and there must always be the possibility of their injecting new information into the situation. If the players are allowed, indeed expected, to invent answers and provide new information, what is to stop them inventing greater and greater powers for themselves and producing fictitious resources to solve their problems? This is the situation sometimes referred to as 'the Armageddon syndrome' where players summon up larger forces in order to overcome their enemies.

The key to the situation as Jones (1980) points out is to ensure that the participants realize that the simulation is not pretend, but real. They are being asked to make decisions and conduct interactions just as they would in real life and, as in real life, the power that they have been given by the role-play designer brings with it the responsibility of working within a real framework. To turn themselves into magicians is no solution to the problems with which they are learning to cope; if learning is to be effective, they must try out their own real skills to solve their problems in the way that they, or the people they are trying to understand, would have to solve them.

HINT Ensure that participants are always checking against what would be likely to happen in real life.

The other thing to bear in mind is that although the players have complete control over their interaction with each other they do not have control over their interaction with the outside world. This interface is represented by the tutor, organizer or controller of the simulation. By adopting various roles – secretary, usher, police officer, reporter, treasurer, politician or even postman – the tutor can exercise positive or negative sanctions over the resources available to the players. Such resources can not only include materials, but also manpower and information. By the judicious use of this technique the tutor can steer players away from potential escalation.

A similar use of role taking by the tutor will deal with the unfortunate situation where he discovers that some vital piece of preparation has been left undone, although too many cases of this will give him a reputation for ingenuity but not enhance his simulations.

In general, if the role-play and the lead-in to it have been properly prepared, the players will be sufficiently informed and motivated to ensure that the enactment proceeds if not smoothly, at least with enthusiasm and drive. Provided that they have sufficient motivation and work together as a group they will rescue each other at those moments when one of them dries up or takes a dead-end path. If the tutor finds that he really has to intervene (and interventions should always be kept to an absolute minimum) then it is usually most acceptable if he does so in a minor role – 'I have been asked to deliver this note to you, sir' – or words to that effect. More important changes to the role-play are best left to a re-enactment, or to the use of one of the other techniques discussed below.

Special techniques

So far we have looked at the two main ways of setting up an average role-play. Now we will look at the other techniques which have been developed for special purposes. A checklist of all the techniques is given in Figure 7.2.

The point of many of these techniques is to enable the role-player to explore the implications of a role more deeply than he would using the straightforward techniques. Many of them were developed in the 1920s by a Viennese psychiatrist, Jacob L Moreno (Moreno, 1953) and have been rediscovered and modified by a variety of people in more recent times. Like many of the group and exploratory techniques discussed in Chapter 9, Moreno's techniques, which he called 'psychodrama', were originally developed for use with patients or clients who needed therapy. They are widely used for this purpose today. Like any tool, however, they may be used in other areas provided the user understands the distinctions and boundaries within which to work. Above all else the tutor must use his professional judgement and resist the temptation to enter into the field of therapy just because he happens to be using particularly powerful exploratory techniques.

Fish-bowl
Multiple
Role-rotation
Role-reversal
Alter ego/Doubling
Mirroring
Supporter
Soliloquy
Chair
Silent auxiliary
Consultant group
Positioning
Replay

Figure 7.2 Techniques in running role-plays

Although each technique was originally developed to bring out a particular aspect of therapy and self-analysis there is nothing sacrosanct about the way in which they may be used. As with any other method, the tutor should experiment with their use as and when he feels his students are able to cope with them. In particular these variations are useful in situations when the player needs the support of one or more fellow students; in other words they may be used to support the shy, the less able or less imaginative student in his role. Obviously, because of their origin, they may also be used to carry exploration of motives, behaviour and expectations further than in the straightforward role-plays.

It is helpful in the description of these techniques to use the terminology which is associated with psychodrama although some of it has overtones which are not intended. The main character in the role-play is called the protagonist. In the type of role-plays used in therapy there is often only one protagonist, the person under therapy; for our purposes, however, there may be several protagonists or people around whom the role-play revolves.

If there are two sides to the issue being explored then the other principal role-player is called the antagonist. The antagonist is the 'significant other' who provides the resistance against which the protagonist pushes his ideas and wishes. The remaining characters who are there to provide background and information are called auxiliaries. Thus, in the simple case of a job interview where the role-play is being used to train the interviewer, the role of the interviewer is the protagonist, that of the interviewee the antagonist, and the roles of the secretary, receptionist, etc the auxiliaries.

We may imagine a more complex role-play designed to elicit feelings about other cultures where all the members of the two cultures may be equally important and are therefore regarded as the protagonists. On the other hand, if we introduce some explorers or missionaries into the simulation and want to investigate their assumptions and attitudes, we would regard them as the protagonists and the 'foreigners' as the antagonists. The word 'antagonist' does not imply anyone actively working against the protagonist, merely someone who is different from him.

In these terms therefore the straight role-play consists of a protagonist meeting with an antagonist or auxiliaries. In multiple role-play there are a number of protagonists, each with their own antagonist, working in parallel.

Role-rotation

The first of the alternative techniques is that of role-rotation. In this the role of the protagonist is rotated between a number of students. Sometimes it may be rotated across all the students so that they have all had experience of playing that part. The rotation is usually done fairly rapidly with each student only playing the part for a few minutes.

This is clearly a useful technique for enabling students to try, or demonstrate, different approaches to the same problem. It gets over the deadening effect of a member of the audience saying 'ah well, you should have done it that way'. It also gives the players time to consider their approach and, because the individual sessions are short, the players are less likely to dry up. This is also a useful technique where the original simulation has taken some time and effort to set up – a committee, public meeting, international dispute, trade fair, workshop manufacturing a product – and where there is one particular role: mediator, counsellor, managing director, which the tutor would like a number of students to experience.

The experience of playing more than one role within the same role-play gives players increased confidence and this leads to greater spontaneity and an enhanced ability to gain insight into, and awareness of, other roles. It can also have the effect of clarifying the situation because the change of role-player leads to slight changes in suppositions and vocabulary which force the players to consider their positions more carefully.

Another type of procedure, also known as role-rotation, is where a number or all of the roles are rotated simultaneously. This is less common because of the obvious complications, but again it enables students to have a go at more than one part and hence to gain an insight into several sides of a dispute or partisan situation. As with the other type of rotational role-play this can avoid the embarrassment of focusing on only one person, and can be used to demonstrate how different people react to the same problem.

In both these variations, however, there is the potential danger of highlighting the fact that one person is clearly the worst at handling the problem. They are also not very suitable for role-plays with large numbers of characters unless some students are prepared to remain as auxiliaries all the time. (Rotational role-play is sometimes known as multiple role-play but in this book we will keep the latter term to denote role-plays that take place in parallel.)

Role-reversal

Another widely-used variation of role-play is the use of role-reversal. There are a number of different ways in which role-reversal may be achieved. In the first case the players who have been cast as protagonist and antagonist – trade unionist and manager, teacher and pupil, customer and salesman – exchange their roles. In another version the student who is playing himself is replaced by another player and so becomes the antagonist. Thus he may take the part of his own boss, wife or golfing partner. In the third version of role-reversal the players are asked to take a part which is outside their normal range of experience because of non-behavioural or physical traits such as sex, racial characteristics, disabilities, etc. Hence we have the situation of a woman playing a man, a white playing a black and so on.

The interesting thing to note is the difference between the way in which the age, sex, race of a player may be ignored in most cases when casting the roles, and the way in which in role-reversal the differences are deliberately seized upon. As indicated in Chapter 5, the writing of a role specification should not go into more detail than necessary. This is particularly the case with physical characteristics. The role may be specified in terms of relationships but these can be kept general such as grandparent, assistant, colleague, and in this way students of either sex, any race or build, etc can play them.

With role-reversal, however, one is trying to show the player what it feels like to be a woman, or blind, or looked down upon or even regarded with awe and respect. It is not necessary to 'put on an act'. All that is needed is for the player to consider carefully what he believes to be the constraints which operate for that role in that situation. If I am a woman, what are the conventions about my approaching a man? If I am a child, what can I reasonably do and not do? Is it normally within the power of a manager to give the trade union representative everything he asks for? What will other people think of me if I do so-and-so?

This is the sort of approach which is needed by the role-reversal player. He is not required to put on a high-pitched voice, to shout, to thump the table. Of course, in the situation that he finds himself in he may discover that the only thing he can do in his frustration is to shout, thump the table, wheedle and coax. But then the actions have arisen as a consequence of the situation, not as a piece of artificial acting. It is under these circumstances that the role-player begins to realize how our actions and behaviour are shaped by the world around us.

There are some circumstances which are ideally suited to using role-reversal techniques and one of these is the exploration and clarification of communication between men and women, particularly in areas of sexual concern. The interchanges which precede sexual advances are usually of a highly ambiguous nature – the boy thinks the girl thinks the boy thinks the girl thinks that ... . Interpretation is based on an understanding of the role acted by the other person and the real meaning of their signals. Convention demands that the man is the initiator; a woman feels that femininity depends on her show of resistance. But society's expectations are changing, and anyway how do you signal 'no' when you mean 'no' if someone else is using the same signals to mean 'maybe'? These issues can be highlighted and explored by using role-reversal techniques.

As indicated above, role-reversal may be used in a variety of settings and for different purposes. One of the most dramatic ways in which it can be used is at the climax of a role-play when each player is emotionally committed to a particular point of view. The effect of having to change this viewpoint can give a powerful impetus to learning about other people's attitudes and the way that a particular situation is seen from both sides.

Special consideration must be given to the situation where players are asked to exchange roles with someone who has technical skills and knowledge which they do not possess. Take for example the training of magistrates. If there is a need to sensitize magistrates to the feelings of a person who is being cross-questioned or sentenced then the role-play can be arranged in a fairly simple way. The magistrates are given simple briefs to role-play offenders; they plead guilty or not guilty and the case is heard in a way familiar to them from the other side of the bench. They will have a mental picture of what they have done, or not done, and will be able to feel the impact of questioning and sentencing accordingly.

If, however, there is a need to sensitize them to the problems of an expert witness in court, the technical knowledge that they will require in the role must be taken into consideration. The way to deal with this is to carefully identify those aspects of the expert witness's skills and knowledge which are relevant to the case, and give role-players a summary of these so that they are in the same position as the witness in terms of the information which is at the front of his mind when dealing with the case.

For example, a case of child care is to be heard and a witness is called to give evidence about child abuse or non-accidental injury. If the witness is a doctor then the role-player must be given precise details of injuries in the correct medical terms. Moreover, he must be briefed on the way in which a doctor would distinguish between the causes of injury and the technical reasons behind this discrimination. Thus equipped, the role-player will be able to put himself in the position of a witness who has the expert knowledge but finds it difficult to communicate it within the constraints of the court.

Alter ego and doubling

The following techniques are a group of variations which depend on the use of other players to reveal aspects of the protagonist that are normally hidden. The first of these is variously known as alter ego or doubling. In this the protagonist and antagonist play their parts as normal but one extra player (or more) is brought in to speak the feelings which he attributes to the players. The auxiliary who is to speak the feelings of the protagonist stands behind the protagonist; the auxiliary revealing the thoughts of the antagonist stands behind the antagonist. Each auxiliary speaks in the first person – 'I just don't believe what you say', 'That was very hurtful', 'Maybe I'm just kidding myself', 'You're not going to get the better of me', 'I'm very angry about this'.

It goes without saying that the person playing the alter ego or double must be sensitive enough to provide feedback without undermining the confidence of the player who is shadowed. It is a technique more suited to adults who have used role-play before than to students or children. It is also better used when the role-play is short or episodic and there are opportunities for the protagonist and double to discuss between themselves how accurately the double is empathizing. On the other hand, it is a technique which in sensitive and experienced hands can bring to the surface the emotional content of a verbal interaction that is so often buried under an articulate exchange. One may even have more than one double for a player and try to get the doubles to act as different aspects of the feelings – the optimistic and pessimistic, for example. This can provide interest, light relief and at the same time, some more insights.

Mirroring

Another technique which requires the use of auxiliary players is mirroring. The idea here is to get another player to re-enact the scene in the role of protagonist whilst the original protagonist watches. In the therapeutic environment of psychodrama this can be a powerful way of showing clients how they appear to others. It is not so likely to have a place in the education and training fields because of the obvious threat which it poses to the individual. Its less threatening manifestation is role-rotation, which we have already discussed.

Supporter

One technique which appears similar to those just outlined is that of the supporter, although it is very different in practice. This technique is designed to help in those situations where either the player dries up or the members of the audience feel that the scene is not going well. The supporter role is that of a person who comes and stands behind the original player and speaks for him. The supporter speaks in the first person, just the same as the protagonist, and comes in at a suitable break point when there is a pause in the speech of the protagonist, or in order to answer the antagonist.

As indicated in the above description, supporters can either help to fill in the gaps or give the role-play new direction. They come from the ranks of the audience, make their contribution and then return. Their contribution may take the form of a single sentence or they may remain in place for several minutes. When they have finished they unobtrusively go back to their seats.

As with the more taxing alter ego procedure, there must be considerable rapport between the player and supporter but the technique is by no means as difficult as it sounds. It can provide a useful alternative to stopping a role-play when the life and direction seems to have gone out of it, yet there is clearly a lot left to be explored. Although in general these techniques are not as fearsome to use as they appear to be when written down, they need to be introduced in a gradual manner to allow students to become accustomed to their use. If the tutor wants to use any of these doubling techniques as an addition to the more straightforward styles of role-play, it is as well to try them out during some warm-up exercises so that the class can get used to ideas which at first are bound to be strange to them.

Soliloquy, chair and silent auxiliaries

Some types of role-play come under the general heading of monodrama. On the whole they are not particularly suitable for educational use but the experienced teacher or trainer should be able to adapt them for his own use in special circumstances. There are three subdivisions of monodrama: soliloquy, a chair auxiliary ego and a silent auxiliary ego.

In the soliloquy the role-player gives himself up to a type of stream of consciousness where he talks out aloud his feelings and attitudes, his decisions and fears. This is not an easy thing to do for most people, but strangely enough it is made a lot easier if there is a physical object to talk to, hence the chair auxiliary ego. A chair is placed in the acting area and the player uses it to represent one or more people with whom he interacts. He talks to and at the chair and responds to the way in which he imagines the other person is responding to him. And it works – at least in the therapeutic setting. This idea may be successfully expanded to use two or more chairs with the protagonist sitting first on one and then on another as he takes the part of each character in turn and talks to the others from that point of view.

The silent auxiliary ego is a variation on this where a person is substituted for the chair. Like the chair, the person playing the auxiliary ego says nothing but is there to support and encourage the protagonist.

Consultant group

There remain three more techniques which may be of use to the role-play tutor. The first of these is the consultant group. This can be used where the role-play is complex or difficult, and where there are a number of ways in which decision-taking may be approached. The technique consists of having a special home support group whose functions are to act as consultants and to advise the protagonist on how to proceed.

Before the role-play begins the players meet with their consultant groups and discuss with them the whole background to the role-play and the way in which they think it should be handled. During the role-play the tutor either arranges for there to be periodic breaks for the consultative meetings to take place or writes the role-play in such a way that the meetings arise as a natural part of the action. One of the great virtues of this technique is its closeness to real life. Everyone has heard of ambassadors being recalled to their governments for consultations and then going back to the negotiating table with a new brief or new information.

HINT Use support groups to plan, monitor, and review the action of players.

The use of these supporting consultative groups has a lot to recommend it. They provide an opportunity for the less articulate to become involved; they give a wider spectrum of experience to draw from; and they act as a non-threatening introduction to the idea of role-play for those in the support group. It can sometimes happen that one of the support group becomes so enthusiastic about his contribution to the discussion that he wants to take over the actual role. By combining the idea of the support group with one of the other techniques which provide for role changes, it is possible to allow for this to happen, and the supporter becomes the role-player for a time.

Another spin-off from the use of the support group is the emphasis which it places on carefully considering a situation before going into it. It is one of the virtues of role-play that it can provide a balance between the emotional, impulsive side of communication and the planned, considered side. The use of the support group technique underlines the importance of preplanning before undertaking such things as interviews, committees and negotiations of all kinds.

People often accuse the tutor of being cold-blooded when he says that every interaction should be planned and prepared for; he may find it difficult to persuade his students of the need to pause and consider at every stage. The experience of support groups can show the practical value of these pauses for thought, and the groups should be encouraged to ask the player questions which help clarify his attitude to the role as well as putting forward their own ideas and suggestions.

Positioning and replay

Finally it is worth mentioning briefly two other aspects of methodology: the deliberate use of physical positioning and the use of replays. A role-play will normally be set up to represent as accurately as possible the physical setting of the scene to be played. In some circumstances, however, it can be advantageous to upset preconceived notions of special relationships by changing the physical positions in which the scene is played. It may be that the boss is standing, whilst the employee is behind the desk; two role-players may be asked to talk several feet away from each other, or extremely close to each other; one player may be told to stand behind the other where he cannot see him. These changes in physical relationships not only demonstrate the importance of space as a factor in communication, but also isolate some aspects of communication such as facial expression, tone of voice and so on.

This deliberate inversion of the norm also forces the role-players to reappraise what they are doing. If they feel less secure when they are taken from behind their desk, or have to sit on the floor to talk up to the other person then how does this affect the way they talk or argue? How important is it to see the other person's face when talking to them, and does this relate to attempts to assess the accuracy or truth of what they are saying? In some role-plays the alternative scenarios come easily to hand: if parents are sitting at the breakfast table when their children come down for breakfast, will they put down their newspapers when they talk? In other cases more manipulation is needed to achieve the required results.

Lastly there is the question of replays. No hard and fast rules can be laid down about these. Obviously if the role-play builds up to an unexpected surprise and vital information is kept concealed until the end then a replay would be of limited value. Conversely, if the role-play is designed to teach simple interpersonal skills then repetition is of the essence. In the majority of cases there is a range of choices open to the tutor. On the whole there is too little rather than too much use made of replay. Time may be short; tutors may be hesitant about boring the class; they may wonder what more could be learnt. But in many cases it would be better to use shorter role-plays and repeat them, or parts of them, rather than to use longer and more elaborate ones once only.

A typical, elaborate business simulation may take the form of a dozen or more students role-playing managers in different hierarchical relationships within a complex company structure. The simulation obliges them to make a number of decisions and to hold a series of meetings. It may take a day or more. At the end of the simulation it is often found that one or two meetings were crucial, and that the decisions taken there were not always rational, or that they suffered through lack of preparation or knowledge. At the same time there are usually periods when some of the players become bored with their roles because the action has moved away from their sector or they are waiting for the result of certain decisions or actions before making their next move. At such times side meetings spring up which give the tutor the impression that everyone is fully involved but which in reality serve no more purpose than a tea-break, chat or walk in the park.

> **TIP** Select the most productive parts of the role-play and replay them with one or two changes in the instructions.

The answer is to analyse the content of the simulation and to split it up into its component parts. Decision-making, the importance and interpretation of company statistics, the need to keep everyone informed, the interdependence of decisions, expressing one's opinions and arguing them through – these are typical of the individual aspects of such a simulation. By using a variety of methods such as case studies, action mazes, group project work, it should be possible to separate out those aspects which can best be illustrated by the use of role-play. Learning the component parts is more efficient and there is more time to repeat the critical sections of role-play if desired. There are strong arguments of course for exposing students to the complexities of the long and sophisticated simulations we have been considering, but not if time is too short to allow for replays where they could be beneficially used.

Replays can take as many forms as there are forms of role-play itself. Roles may be reversed or rotated, auxiliary players used, new instructions issued, the physical layout altered, or the observers' brief changed. On the other hand it may be sufficient to repeat the role-play under exactly the same conditions as before. The only important point is that the tutor should consider the use of replay and the possibility of changing the format of the role-play for the replay.

The tutor's role

During the actual running of the role-play the tutor has to perform a number of different functions which change as the role-play progresses. These are listed in Figure 7.3.

Choose the type

The first and vital function of the tutor is to decide on the type of role-play to be used and then to keep an eye on it to ensure that the performance is not diverted from the intended style. Of course, the

> 1. Choose and facilitate techniques
> 2. Provide information
> 3. Adjudicate
> 4. Control time
> 5. Engender energy
> 6. Correct problems
> 7. Not act as a therapist

Figure 7.3 The tutor's role

style itself need not be rigidly fixed to one of the types discussed in Chapter 4. Although these typologies are a convenient way of classifying role-plays for the purposes of deciding how to go about them, in practice the divisions are blurred and styles may be deliberately changed as the players become more immersed in the role-play. It also follows that the choice of technique is not restricted to just one of those discussed earlier in this chapter. It is possible to incorporate several aspects of the techniques into one role-play For example, a fish-bowl format may be used with some of the observers also acting as consultant groups within which a particular person might be chosen to act as supporter or as a double. It is even possible to have a supporter and a double for the same player.

Provide information

The tutor must also provide information and adjudicate in disputes. In the ideal situation he will not need to act during the running of the role-play itself because all the information has been distributed in the form of briefing notes or mechanisms within the exercise itself. Wherever possible the information should include sufficient guidelines to avoid disputes over facts, including the distribution of authority within the role-play.

> **TIP** Establish the ground rules for the session by discussion with the participants. Consider actually writing them down.

Adjudicate

Sometimes, however, it may be necessary for the tutor to intervene because of unexpected developments. In this case he should intervene in role as far as possible, choosing a 'gate-keeper' role from which to operate. The term 'gate-keeper' in this sense means a person who, by virtue of his position, controls the flow of information and, by extension, orders or instructions, from the outside. Examples of this role are receptionists, secretaries, government spokesmen, reporters and librarians. Although the role-bearers themselves may not have authority, they can draw attention to laws or regulations at will.

The tutor must be very careful to ensure that interruptions and interjection of new material are justified. Certainly he should not interrupt to correct the players unless this is imperative. It is better to wait until the debriefing and let students learn by their mistakes than to disrupt the proceedings. Such a disruption will not only demoralize the students but prevent them from progressing from the first stage of being a player to the second stage of getting into role. The first stage is one of acting superficially; the second is a deeper empathy with the role that leads to real understanding and change of attitude. It has been said that one of the keys to the successful running of a role-play is the willpower of the tutor to resist the temptation to correct faults and otherwise interfere.

Control time

The role of the tutor as a time-keeper is obvious. Again it is a function which can often be built into the role-play but when this is not possible you may perform the function within role if you want to finish the role-play in a natural way. Sometimes tutors will want to stop the role-play from outside so that they can discuss some points and start it up again. This is much easier to do than most tutors imagine. In general, students are sufficiently flexible to allow the role-play to be stopped for discussion and restarted again without losing too much. In some cases this may even be done several times at frequent intervals.

A common phenomenon known to psychologists is the end effect. If people know that their task is going to finish in a few minutes' time this affects a variety of functions such as risk-taking, speed of action and so on. It may be that the tutor wants to avoid this end effect. The commonest ways of doing this are either to leave the finishing time deliberately ambiguous or vague or to announce a false finishing time and then cut the session short – an unfortunate but necessary deceit in cases where it is important to avoid the end effect.

Engender energy

There are sometimes occasions when the role-play seems to be grinding to a halt for no apparent reason. It is not that the players are getting bored, or the play becoming repetitive – there just seems to be a staleness creeping in. It is the type of situation which is considerably easier to observe than to describe. On these occasions the job of the tutor is to inject zest into the proceedings, to animate them. There is no golden prescription for these occasions; so much depends on the personality of the tutor. Somehow he must find ways of conveying his enthusiasm and energy to the group. Whether this is done by entering into the role-play, by means of a pep-talk or by non-verbal signs of enthusiasm, the main prerequisite is for the tutor himself to be enthusiastic. Unfortunately no book can turn an unenthusiastic tutor into an enthusiastic one.

Avoid therapy

The last but no less important function for the tutor is to 'trouble-shoot'. This is discussed in the next section, but before proceeding to it a warning note should be sounded. The functions described above will all be part of a tutor's job when running role-plays. It is not part of the tutor's normal job to act as a therapist. There are close similarities between the way in which role-play is used in education and training and the way in which it is used in therapeutic situations. After all, therapy is an educative process and changing people's behaviour and attitudes often implies the removal of undesirable behaviour or attitudes. The process of therapy, however, requires different knowledge, different skills and a different context. The suppositions on both sides are different and, in particular, the responsibilities are allocated in a different way. The temptation to play God must be firmly resisted.

Intervention and involvement

Coming out of role

One of the commonest problems when running a role-play is the student who persists in coming 'out-of-role' in order to explain why he is doing a particular thing. The dialogue might go something like this:

'Will you support us in our proposal?'
'No I won't – Well I don't think I would have done in those circumstances, do you?'

This is usually a nervous reaction caused by anxiety. It indicates that the warm-up period was not long enough or effective. The immediate solution must be to stop the enactment and discuss the problem with the players. The tutor should point out the advantages of doing rather than saying what could be done. Using one of the support methods discussed earlier in this chapter may help as well. If the problem persists then roles should be rotated and the more nervous players given roles which are easier to encompass. This will give them the experience to take larger roles at a later date.

Another way of dealing with this problem is to encourage players to act as they genuinely feel they want to act, not as they think someone else would. This is because the blockage can occur when the role-player is trying to do two things at the same time: deal with the problem situation as presented to him in the role-play and change behaviour to accord with what he thinks the character involved would do. In most cases the two pieces of behaviour are essentially the same only role-players do not realize it. The important thing is to get them to respond to the stimuli in the setting in which they find themselves. The 'characterization' of the part is icing on the cake and can be put aside as a distraction.

> *Problem areas*
> 1. Player departs from role
> 2. Burlesquing
> 3. Poor performance. Drying up
> 4. Lack of insight/empathy
> 5. Repetition and boredom
> 6. Emotional escalation

Figure 7.4 Intervention and involvement

Burlesquing

Coming out of role is the first problem area listed in Figure 7.4; the second item is burlesquing. This is the equivalent of the student acting the fool in class but is a little more subtle because the border-line between strong involved behaviour and burlesquing is so thin. If the student seems to be 'going over the top', however, the role-play will have to be stopped for the sake of the other players and something done about it. Whether or not this is easy to deal with depends on the students' motivation and whether they are overacting because of genuine overenthusiasm or misunderstanding. If this is the case then the tutor can point out the difference between having to make real decisions in the role-play and acting artificially. If the overacting is more deliberate then clearly a change of role is called for. In both cases a change of environment may help; the physical surroundings such as furniture and equipment may be altered to encourage a more realistic approach and to remove the 'classroom' atmosphere which may encourage rebellion. Providing the players with more work to do in the course of the role-play can also be very beneficial. They may be asked to keep records, do calculations, make decisions or similar tasks to keep them usefully occupied.

Drying up

The opposite of burlesquing could be the student who gives a very poor performance or dries up completely. The best solution to this problem, apart from changing the role-player with potential loss of face, is to use the supporter idea where players have another person to help them at awkward moments. Sometimes it is even possible to change the role so as to share it between two or more characters who act as a group. A customs official can be made into a group of three officials, for example, or an applicant for social welfare benefits into a man and wife, or two friends. This takes the pressure off the individual to respond every time and makes it more like a game of tennis doubles where the action moves from one player to another.

Other ways of dealing with the problem are to use multiple role-playing or to stop the role-play for a while to explore the reasons behind the drying up. In some cases, for example, it may be that the player does not understand the role or lacks the necessary information to respond quickly. The occurrence of a blockage in the role-play may in fact be a good indicator of a problem area. The tutor can turn this to his advantage by using it as a teaching point and exploring the reasons behind it. This is particularly the case if the tutor suspects that the student has not grasped the essentials of the situation or if the role-play has developed in an unexpected way.

Insight and empathy

Lack of insight and empathy with the character being played can be difficult to deal with if it indicates a general lack of sensitivity on the part of the player. The best way of increasing this sensitivity is to use role-reversal and put the player in the opposite part so that he can see the situation from the other point of view.

Boredom

When repetition sets in or boredom becomes evident, the tutor should either change the format of the enactment or stop it altogether. It is an indication that the role-play has run its natural course and is no longer a challenge to the participants. Perhaps in future use the briefs should incorporate more conflict, or the input to the role-play should contain more unexpected material. At all events it is better to finish the role-play than allow it to drag out to a pre-arranged conclusion just to keep to a particular schedule. Stopping the role-play at this point enables one to go back to it as a technique without having alienated the students.

Emotional escalation

The last item in Figure 7.4 is called emotional escalation. It is a problem which worries two groups of tutors using role-play: those who are new to the technique and those who are trying to push it to its educational and training limits without wanting to overstep those limits. Those who are new to role-play worry about it because they realize the close relationship between therapeutic role-play and educational role-play or because they have seen films or television programmes in which what appeared to be role-play techniques produced emotional outbursts far in excess of anything which they would wish to deal with. Those who are experienced may want to experiment with new techniques and do a balancing act between using more powerful methods and getting into a situation which goes beyond their control.

Emotion may be generated during the role-play or in the course of debriefing and the two situations require different approaches. If the emotional temperature rises during the role-play itself then the greatest safeguard is for the tutor to be aware of the potential developments, and sensitive to the way in which things are going. If the players are becoming too agitated and are likely to get carried away in their parts to such an extent that either they or their colleagues would suffer, then the role-play should be stopped and time allowed for defusing the situation.

The point at which this becomes necessary is a matter of judgement which will depend on the tutor's knowledge of the players and their behaviour. It will also depend on the relationships between the students and between students and tutor. Alternatively, roles may be switched or the players re-briefed with a discussion on the purpose of the role-play and the place of emotion within it. It should be borne in mind that the display of emotion is rarely damaging in itself – on the contrary it can be cathartic – it is the potential loss of dignity, or the emotional feeling which is only partly worked out that can cause the damage. Some role-plays can become extremely heated, but with no adverse effects on the students.

HINT Sensitivity and decisiveness are the best safeguards against allowing role-plays to get out of hand.

The other occasion when emotion may be generated is the debriefing. This is because the players may be subjected to penetrating questioning about the causes of their behaviour. This is less likely to be a problem with young children than with adolescents or adults since young children on the whole have not learnt to conceal deep emotion as much as adults have. The degree of probing is largely in the hands of tutors either because they are asking the questions or because they can control the questions which are being asked. The subject is touched on again in the next chapter which deals specifically with debriefing. Here it is sufficient to point out that it is relatively easy to control the emotional climate in debriefing by moderating the amount of negative criticism and impersonalizing comment by directing it at the character rather than the player. The important thing is for tutors to be aware of the temptation to go deeper than they had at first intended, and to resist that temptation in the interests of the student and the group.

! WARNING !

Always question your motives for asking personal questions. Are they for educational or training objectives, or just curiosity?

As a general rule many tutors will try to deal with problems that occur by entering into the role-play themselves and dealing with the problem from within a role. Although this has the undoubted advantage of keeping the role-play going and demonstrating the tutor's belief in the seriousness and importance of the role-play, the inexperienced tutor may find it difficult to do. It is in any case partly a matter of personal style and not everyone would agree that it is necessarily the best method although it is one which the author uses in moderation.

HINT Stopping and re-starting role-play is much easier than you think. After all, people easily go in and out of role in real life.

The running of a role-play makes considerable demands on the tutor. Towers (1969) says that the tutor must possess 'tact, receptivity, skill in communication, insight, imagination, flexibility in dealing with unexpected developments'; no doubt the reader can add more. These skills are equally needed during the debriefing phase but there are a number of ways in which a systematic approach will help. This approach is described in the next chapter.

8 *Debriefing*

The importance of debriefing

We have now reached the box on the flow chart in Figure 8.1 marked 'Debrief'. The end appears to be in sight. At this point many inexperienced tutors tend to relax and allow a short, loosely structured discussion to take place; everyone agrees how interesting the experience of role-play was, and that is the end of the process. The tutor goes away with a feeling of a job well done, the students go away with a feeling of having tried something a little different and a sense of refreshment.

Unfortunately they have missed the point that the debriefing session is the most important part of the activity. It is here that the meaning of the enactment is clarified; the lessons to be learnt are underlined; and the connections are made to what the students already know and what they need for the future.

> **HINT** Debriefing can be the most important part of the exercise. Why not consider it earlier in the planning stage?

The list of purposes given in Figure 8.2 will give some idea of the range and importance of the activity known as debriefing. It is interesting to note that it goes under a variety of names, each of which indicates a different aspect of the process. The word 'debriefing' implies a reversal of the process of briefing – there is a clear connection made between the information put into the role-play and the information extracted from it. Another term which is used is 'reflection', implying an opportunity for participants to look back over the events, and a third is 'discussion' meaning an investigation or

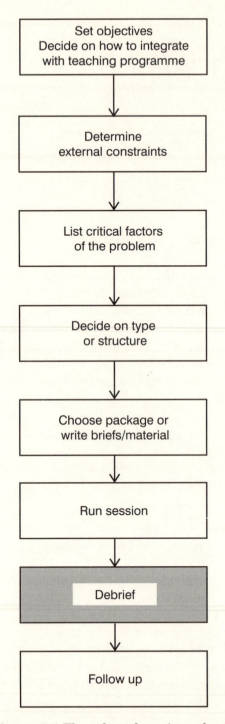

Figure 8.1 Flow chart for using role-play

examination by argument. As indicated in Chapter 3, the term 'debriefing' has been retained as being the one most commonly used. It also has the virtue of emphasizing the connection between the initial objectives which were set and the review of the eventual outcome. Whatever the term used, however, there is no doubt that there must be a well-organized, carefully supervised session in which the purposes tabulated in Figure 8.2 are fulfilled.

1. Bring players out of role.

2. Clarify what happened (on factual level).

3. Correct misunderstandings and mistakes.

4. Dissipate tension/anxiety.

5. Bring out assumptions, feelings and changes which occurred during run.

6. Give players opportunity to develop self-observation.

7. Develop observational skills.

8. Relate outcome to original aims.

9. Analyse why things happened that way.

10. Draw conclusions about behaviour.

11. Reinforce or correct learning.

12. Draw out new points for consideration.

13. Deduce ways of improving behaviour.

14. Apply to other situations.

15. Link with previous learning.

16. Provide plan for future learning.

Figure 8.2 The purpose of debriefing

Function

The reason why debriefing is so often inadequately carried out is that the tutor is unaware of the range of functions which it performs. Obviously a key function will be to draw out the points of learning and ensure that the student has grasped them, but there are a number of other functions of almost equal importance to be carried out.

The enactment of a good role-play produces a high degree of involvement in the players; indeed one of the signs of success is the extent of this involvement. Having encouraged players to immerse themselves in the situation one must devote some time to helping them to withdraw from it again. In this we are not referring to the temporary pause for consideration and analysis that might take place during the enactment – the 'time out' that may be used as an opportunity to re-assess the situation. We are speaking here of the final withdrawal of the players from the action. This withdrawal must be made clear and absolute, otherwise the tutor will find that students' attention is diverted on to unresolved problems within the role-play.

After a role-play it is common for the players to want to go on discussing and arguing about what actually took place. In effect they often want to re-enact the situation to try out other approaches or responses. If they are not happy about the way the role-play is resolved they will continue to have it nagging at the back of their minds.

To avoid this problem the tutor must first make sure that misunderstandings are cleared up and loose ends tied. In addition there must be a logical process of stepping back from the role-play by treating the players as if they were still involved in their characters and then successively moving to engage them as students again. During this process the tutor can move from bringing out any emotional feelings which the player had in character to a more objective discussion of the issues.

This disengagement of the participants from the role-play itself has a second and equally important function. Role-playing and analysis are incompatible behaviours. One requires total immersion in the problem, the other a deliberate stepping back. At the debriefing stage the participants need to be able to step back and analyse what has been going on. In order to do so they must first feel that they have finished, rounded off their previous activity.

Another functional area to be covered by debriefing relates to skills of observation. Role-play usually provides an opportunity to develop the skill of observing oneself and others, and the debriefing period provides the chance to reinforce those skills and correct errors.

The other major function of the debriefing should be to link the role-play with the rest of the teaching. This can be done both by looking back to the original aims and forward towards applications of the learning in other situations, and the following up of interesting points by further teaching or research.

Although the remainder of this chapter deals with debriefing after the role-play, it is worth emphasizing that some very useful feedback can often be built into the role-play itself by using such mechanisms as reporters, radio programmes, memos, reports and newspaper stories.

When, where and how long

In order to have the maximum effect, the debriefing session must follow soon after the enactment itself. Since participants will be trying to recall their attitudes, feelings and responses it will help if there is not too great a time lapse between finishing the role-play and beginning the debriefing.

In practice of course it is not always easy to arrange this. Meal-times, coffee breaks, and even bedtimes are likely to intervene. The important thing, however, is to plan the debriefing carefully and to allow sufficient time. Most authors agree that the time for debriefing should be at least as long as the actual role-play; in practice it is desirable to allow two to three times as long. Thus a typical role-play lasting for quarter of an hour should be given about three-quarters of an hour for adequate debriefing. Longer role-plays will require proportionately longer to debrief.

There comes a time, however, when the total length of time for the exercise becomes too great. At this point the proportions are likely to change. If the role-play lasts for more than half an hour, it is going to make very heavy weather to continue the debriefing for more than an additional hour and a half. In these cases it is advisable to reconsider the exercise and to see whether it could be changed into a series of shorter episodes.

The essential point is that poor planning will almost inevitably lead to a premature end. Time will run out at an arbitrary point in the discussion and may not only curtail the most important part of the learning process but also miss critical points which would have emerged at the end.

It is often not realized how much material can be accumulated in a relatively short time. For instance, take the case of a role-play involving a head of department who is approached by one of her staff wanting a transfer to another department.

Within five or ten minutes they may have touched on the work-load of the member of staff, how it relates to that of other members of staff, whether she is capable of undertaking that level of work, what the working atmosphere is like, whether she wants to move as part of career development, for financial reasons, because of her colleagues, because of the work itself, etc. And any of these may lead to deeper enquiry without even touching on home circumstances and all that surrounds them. After a short time, therefore, it should be possible to ask the role-players 'How do you feel about the interview?', 'What have you found out?', 'What is your attitude to the other person?', 'Have your feelings, attitudes changed?', 'Do you feel the other person understands your problems?', 'Do you understand theirs?', 'Why did you ask about hours of work?'

As a result of this discussion it may be decided to:

- continue the interview;
- start again;
- re-run or continue the role-play but with changed parameters;
- stop and go on to the next part of the session.

If the role-play had been continued for half an hour the participants would have forgotten what the first few minutes were like and a lot of the detail might have been lost. Similarly, if there was a considerable break between the enactment and debriefing, the memory of detail and of feelings would fade.

Another way to ensure a clear picture is to hold the discussion in the same room, even where there has been a break. Physical surroundings have a noticeable effect on people's powers of recollection, and to place someone in the same room, the same chair, the same position, will often stimulate their memory of earlier incidents.

It is of course possible to use closed circuit television (CCTV) and to record the role-play. The replaying of the videotape will then refresh people's memory of the events thus partly avoiding the problem of having to arrange the debriefing immediately after the enactment. This can be a useful and powerful way of using CCTV. There are also a number of disadvantages to its use and these are discussed at the end of this chapter.

The logic of debriefing

Although every tutor will have their own style of teaching and hence their own style of conducting a debriefing session, it is helpful to keep in mind a picture of the overall logic of the process. This is illustrated in Figure 8.3.

As can be seen from the table, the process falls into four distinct sections. There are those activities which are designed to complete the enactment and role-playing itself so that the teaching environment returns to its original state. Then there is the central activity of discussion and analysis in order to form conclusions and register them as facts to be remembered. After that comes the follow through which is essential if the session is not to be left in isolation from the rest of the programme of teaching and instruction. Lastly there is the need to provide encouragement and support so that the student can pursue the new ideas which have been inspired by the role-play.

Another way of expressing this is to say that one should first question the content of the role-play and then the process. It can be seen that this is the logical path to take because a lengthy discussion could easily lead nowhere if there was a fundamental misunderstanding of the content of what took place.

In a way one could argue that this is the logical structure for the winding up of any teaching or training session. It takes on extra significance for role-play sessions, however, because not only is the finishing stage of a role-play session a greater proportion of the total than normal but the students are likely to want, either consciously or unconsciously, to remain within the environment of the role-play which has motivated them so much.

The sequence of debriefing

Using the logic described above the tutor can now easily construct a set of steps to be followed in the debriefing session. This can be

Clear up role-play

Establish facts, clear up misunderstandings, debug.
Find out how players saw themselves and others.
Bring players out of role.
Find out what observers saw happen.
Interpret actions in terms of role-play assumptions.

Draw conclusions

Decide why things happened.
Analyse interactions.
Establish sequences, causes, effects.
Extrapolate to the real world.
Draw generalized conclusions.

Develop action plan
Within the classroom

Repeat role-play with variations.
Develop new exercises.
Follow up with further instruction.

Outside the classroom

Change ways of behaving/working.
Find ways of improving things.

Provide support

Be ready with advice, help, resources.

Figure 8.3 The logic of debriefing

particularly useful where the class has been divided into groups which role-play the same scenario in parallel with one another. In this case the tutor is likely to want a sizeable part of the debriefing, or even the whole of it, to be carried out in the separate groups since much of it will be particular to an individual group's enactment. This means that the critical job of facilitating the debriefing has to be done by selected students. It is most useful to give them a clear sequence of steps to follow in order that the maximum benefit is obtained whilst ensuring that the individuals concerned feel they have been given a fair hearing and that there is no residual stress or strain.

As indicated above, this sequence can be a personal one devised by the tutor. Indeed it is possible to go so far as to write out the exact questions to be asked and to have them typed on a set of prompt cards for the tutor or the group leaders to use. The wording of the questions will naturally vary according to the actual role-play and the needs of the tutor. Most sequences, however, will follow a similar pattern, and this general sequence is illustrated in the flowchart in Figure 8.4. It takes the group through a process of unwinding, reorganizing and crystallizing into new pieces of learning and future plans. This corresponds to the general process of any change, known by social psychologists as the unfreezing of behaviour patterns, moving to new patterns and re-freezing the new patterns into place.

In addition to following the right sequence, the tutor must also adapt the style of questioning to each stage in the sequence. Both the type of question and the relationship of the tutor and student must change during the process if it is to be conducted efficiently.

We next look at the stages in debriefing and then at the techniques which can be used for each phase.

The three phases of questioning

Phase 1 – Establishing the facts

The tutor should start by explaining how the debriefing session is going to be organized; the logic and sequence. This is also the opportunity for making some complimentary remarks about the way in which participants worked at the exercise. It is important to start on a positive note.

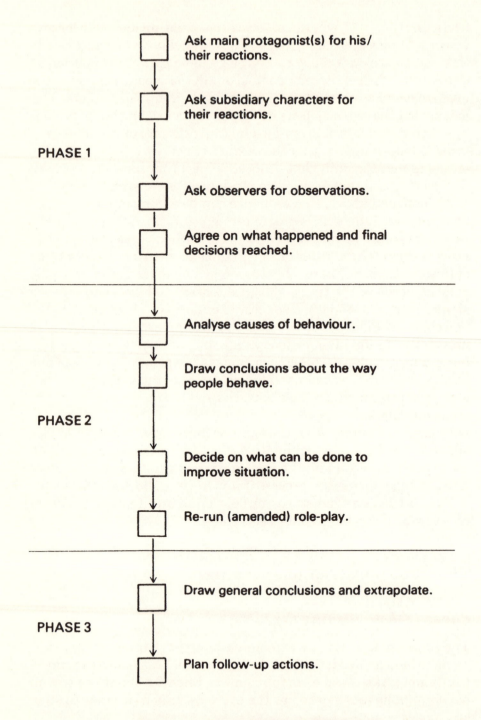

Figure 8.4 Flow chart for debriefing

After that, the first person to talk should always be the main protagonist – the person around whom the problem or event is built. Not only are they a key person from the point of view of the problem which is being explored, but they are likely to be the person who is most under emotional stress because of being the focus of attention.

> **TIP** Get players to stay in, or take up, the physical positions they occupied during role-play. This aids the memory.

The protagonist(s) should be given the opportunity to make observations about themselves first, before anyone else does. If other people make critical observations about their behaviour, this will tend to put them on the defensive. They will 'clam up', and the free flow of discussion will have been lost for good.

In this first round of comment the protagonists should seek to establish a number of points.

What they thought happened.
How they felt about their own decisions.
What they thought the other characters were doing.
How far they felt they had achieved their objectives (and what their objectives were).
What their attitude was towards others.
How far their attitudes, feelings, understanding had changed.

> **TIP** Refer to the participants by their role titles eg 'Quality Controller (or Mr/Ms Smith) – what were you feeling at that point?', or 'As the Quality Controller, what......'.

Clearly the tutor cannot be too rigid about following this framework, but it is best to avoid moving into the 'why' phase at this point. As far as possible the discussion should be focused on what the players thought happened and what their feelings were. The concentration should be on facts and it should be descriptive not evaluative; the temptation to interpret other people's reactions must be resisted and the tutor should discourage any attempt to 'explain' other people's behaviour. Feedback should not be dogmatic or over-generalized.

This phase should enable the players to continue to think in terms of their role, but at a less intense level. This helps the process of gradually easing out of role and into the position of an objective analyst. It also ensures that all the ends are tidied up within the role-play itself, ie that players are not left in mid-air without knowing exactly what everyone thought had happened.

This may seem a strange point to emphasize but many tutors will know how easy it is for misunderstandings to remain, even after views have been exchanged. Take a role-play between two people discussing the level of compensation for injury at work. They arrive at a point where one of them says 'I feel that no amount of money can compensate for the loss of a limb', the other replies 'Yes, I entirely agree with that'. They then carry on discussing how compensation payments can be administered under the illusion that they have both got the same viewpoint.

In the post-enactment discussion the tutor, who has spotted the potential problem, asks 'What did you mean when you said that no amount of money could compensate for the loss of a limb?' The first player says 'I felt that we should devote our energies to increasing the financial compensation to its absolute maximum', the other player says 'I felt that financial compensation, although necessary, could never be the most important thing; what we should do is to deal with financial matters quickly and get on to the crux of the matter which is to provide psychological and physical support services'. If this misunderstanding is not cleared up in the early stages the subsequent discussion would be less effective.

It is also very useful at this stage to bring out changes of attitude which occurred during the run. It is helpful to know how much players were influenced by what was going on and the extent to which their arguments or actions changed other players' beliefs. Also, it can be confusing to be relating statements made at one point in the role-play to the speaker's apparent attitudes at another point if these attitudes have in fact changed unknown to the others.

After the principal characters have had their say, other minor characters should be asked how they saw their behaviour. Only after this opportunity for letting off steam should the observers be asked for their views. It is particularly useful if they can quote a few things that were actually said since this helps to emphasize the factual nature of this phase.

The questions put to the observers will differ according to the particular case being observed. If the purpose of the role-play is to develop structured skills then the observers should follow closely the sequence of actions or instructions and relate their comments to the key steps or guidelines being taught, and the question of whether or not these guidelines are being correctly followed. In the case of less structured, ie developmental, role-play the tutor can be more general and say to the observers 'list the three things you feel helped the interview to run successfully', for example.

Every effort should be made during this phase to make comment as positive as possible. Emphasis should be on what was done rather than what was not done. The latter will creep into the discussion anyway, without the tutor making a meal of it. Credit and praise should be given as well as criticism – an obvious point but one which is neglected by many teachers and trainers in the context of role-play. The student needs encouragement in this activity as much as, or even more than, in more conventional classroom work.

Finally, the tutor, who up until this point has remained strictly in the background, will summarize and get agreement from everyone on the outlines of what happened. The stage is set for phase 2.

Phase 2 – Analysing the causes of behaviour

At this point the role of the tutor changes. He will now be trying to get the group to analyse the interactions that took place and to explore the reasons for certain pieces of behaviour. Students will be encouraged to abandon their attachment to their roles and to start looking at the role-play from the outside.

TIP Move players into different physical locations in the room to emphasise a change in approach. Get them to turn to their neighbour, give their real name, and chat for a minute or two.

During this phase the tutor can bring his own knowledge and experience into play. He can try to get the students to see the experience they have had through a particular framework and hence to analyse their behaviour objectively. It is also a time to encourage the students to draw analogies with their own experience and that of others.

It is now permissible for players to say what they would have done if they were in the other person's shoes and why. On the other hand it is not very productive to argue about how people felt. It must be accepted that people felt how they said they felt, however unlikely it may appear to the other players. If, for example, the person playing the part of a shop steward, who has been shouting at the manager, says that she felt friendly towards him, it is no use arguing that she could not possibly have done so. It is better to accept the statement and discuss why she shouted, or what she means when she says that she felt friendly or unfriendly.

> **TIP** You can now refer to participants by their own names. 'John, when the Quality Controller, who you played, said that, what was the effect on the committee?'.

The tutor is firmly in charge at this point and directs the discussion in order to arrive at general conclusions about the way that people behave in similar situations to the one just enacted, and what can be done to improve the way the situation develops. If necessary the role-play, or parts of it, can be run again with suitable modifications.

When the tutor feels that the lessons of the role-play have been grasped (or when time begins to run out!) it is time to go on to phase 3.

Phase 3 – Planning action

Just as the move from phase 1 to phase 2 involved a change in emphasis from student control to tutor control, so the move from phase 2 to phase 3 should put the onus back on to the student.

The purpose of this phase is to get the student's commitment to some sort of action, whether a change of behaviour, further practice of a skill, or finding out about certain aspects of the subject.

The first stage is to reach agreement on how the findings of the group about behaviour within the role-play and similar situations can be extrapolated to other situations in the real world. Say, for instance, that the role-play has been concerned with the running of a farmers' cooperative in West Africa. It has already been agreed that the obstructive behaviour of one of the players prevented the co-operative from operating well. It has further been agreed that this might be a common problem whenever a group try to come to agreement over the way goods and work are shared out.

The group can now discuss what mechanisms might come into play in real life that would encourage cooperation or disrupt it. They will have examples of real cooperatives which have worked, and others which have not. The special circumstances of the farmers in West Africa can be considered together with social, economic and political influences. From all this it may be possible to decide how realistic the role-play was, and what lessons can be drawn from it about the real world outside. Even a role-play that goes in the opposite way to what the tutor expected will provide material for this phase.

As a result of this discussion the tutor should aim to draw out some plans for action on the part of the student or whole group. Having established what needs to be done next, the tutor must finally ensure that the students have access to the resources they require to carry out their assignments, whether materials, equipment, books or the tutor himself.

One of the possible actions which is worth bearing in mind is a re-run of all or part of the role-play. If the action has been analysed in detail and some of it subjected to criticism, it is almost certain that some of the role-players will be left with a feeling that they would like to have the opportunity to do part of it again. This is not unlike real life; the glorious difference between life and role-play, however, is that in the latter one can try again and prove that it is possible to improve skills and techniques. This opportunity is sometimes thrown away for the sake of saving a few minutes. Where possible the tutor should always offer the role-players the chance to go over a part of the scene again, perhaps with some variation built in to test out an idea. This can dissipate some of the tension and frustration which inevitably surround a less than successful attempt to cope with a situation.

Techniques

Phase 1 – What happened?

The three phases of debriefing each require a rather different technique on the part of the tutor. The techniques themselves are well known to many who use group work as part of their teaching, but it is worth pointing out their use in this context. Debriefing is also unusual in that it requires a change in technique in the course of the session. There is no suggestion that these changes have to be sudden or abrupt; normally the tutor will go from one to the other in a subtle way unnoticed by the students. On the other hand there should be a definite boundary in the mind of the tutor so that the questioning can change to the most effective form for the particular phase. A summary of these techniques is given in Figure 8.5.

In phase 1 the emphasis is on the reaction and feelings of the individual role-player. The tutor's role is to keep well in the background. Therefore the questioning must be open-ended with ample opportunity for the student to express himself. There should be no pressure, and silence must be tolerated to allow time for thought. If there is doubt about an answer, or clarification is needed, the technique of reflection can be used. This is done by reflecting the statement in the form of a question, 'You were puzzled?' It is important to avoid any suggestion of criticism or judgement about the role-play itself unless this was an integral part of the teaching such as specific skills training, neither should rewards be given for beautiful acting.

It should be possible to distinguish between the criticism or praise of performance skill, and comment on the aspects of the role-play from which the student and other members of the group can learn about the problem or subject under investigation.

Some tutors prefer to use small groups wherever possible on the grounds that people feel much less threatened by talking in a small group rather than in a large class. A technique for doing this is to get the players to fill in a reaction sheet and to use this as a basis for small group discussion. Suitable phrases for completion might be:

- The thing that helped me most/least was...
- At the beginning/end I felt ...
- My objectives were ...

Phase 1

Use open-ended questions. How? Why? What?

Concentrate on individual players.

Explore alternative actions.

Reflect feelings.

Insist on descriptive not evaluative comments.

Give feedback in terms of observer's own experience rather than someone else's.

Use group discussion of reaction sheets.

Do not evaluate quality of performance.

Do not argue about misunderstood instructions.

Do not assign motives or make judgements about underlying attitudes.

Emphasize what was done rather than what could have been done.

Use role-titles in discussion, not the player's name.

Phase 2

Ask for reasons. Why? How? Who?

Probe answers. Why not? What if?

Seek alternative theories. Is there another possibility?

Collect other examples. Where else has this happened?

Test conclusions against alternatives. Which makes more sense?

Give views of outside experts.

Phase 3

Get students to commit themselves to actions.

Write up actions on wall posters.

Organize students into action groups or pairs.

Put time scale on actions.

Agree criteria for success.

Figure 8.5 Techniques of debriefing

- Disagreements were dealt with by ...
- Suspicion and resistance were caused by...

Alternatively a set of direct questions can be used.

One policy which is recommended by some authors is to use the role-titles during this part of the discussion rather than the student's name. Thus one would ask 'What did the postman do at that point?', or 'Why did Mrs Taylor, the probation officer, ask for more information at that point?', or 'Mrs Taylor, tell us why you asked for information then?' or 'How did Johnson (the manager) feel about that?' The advantage of this style is that the student does not feel put under the spotlight as a person. The person who is being interrogated is the character in the role-play. Furthermore it enables the tutor to signal the change to phase 2 in a distinct way when he begins to ask questions directed at the students by name.

Phase 2 – Why did it happen?

In phase 2 the character of questioning can become more demanding and analytical. It is during this phase that the tutor can take command as a person of knowledge and experience. The style of questioning should be aimed at encouraging the student to make connections with other experiences and with some of the theoretical background to the work. Questions can be direct and closed, ie 'Should the chairman have decided in that way?' or 'Who was the person who was leader?'. As the questioning proceeds the student should be encouraged to look for alternative explanations and examples.

At all times during debriefing the tutor must remember that it should be tailored to the specific needs of the individual students, the group, and the particular teaching task. This is why generalized lists of questions are only of limited use. This concentration on the specific aims of the session is particularly important during phase 2. It focuses attention on the subject area and its problems.

Phase 3 – What do we do next?

Phase 3 may not always be possible. It is a phase in which the tutor endeavours to get a forward commitment by the students to some forms of action. Here the emphasis is on getting a public declaration in writing of what they intend to do. That way they are more likely to keep to their intentions. It is as well to establish what evidence they will produce to show that they have done what they intended to do.

During phases 2 and 3 many of the standard teaching techniques which assume teacher leadership and control can be used. The tutor may want to incorporate illustrative material or expand on certain points. In particular the use of a flip chart to record some of the analytical points made in phase 2 and the intentions expressed in phase 3 can be very productive. Not only does it provide a focus for discussion and a means of pacing the contributions and allowing for natural pauses, it also acts as a record which can be referred to when following up at a later date.

HINT Do not underestimate the potential of the humble flip chart.

Figure 8.6 provides a checklist of points to take into consideration when planning debriefing.

---

1. Allow sufficient time.
2. Arrange room for discussion focused on participants.
3. Ensure each role-player has an opportunity to speak.
4. Check that you have understood the feelings of each person.
5. Keep a written record of points.
6. Draw up list of main conclusions.
7. Consider re-running the role-play with variations.
8. Agree the next step with the students.
9. Make sure that students have understood how their experiences relate to the real world.

Figure 8.6 Checklist for debriefing

There is perhaps a final point worth making. The reader may have got the impression from the above advice that the author is suggesting that students should be kept working strenuously all the time. This was not the intention. The argument is more for a structure and rationale to the activity rather than a continuous pressure. On the contrary, there is much to be said for a certain amount of relaxation and informality during debriefing. The body cannot distinguish between real and false emotion, or between real and pretend crises. If the role-players have become immersed in their parts their bodies will have been subjected to almost as much stress as they would have been in real life. It is quite likely that they will be mentally and physically exhausted and need a period of relaxation before the next job they have to tackle. The ideal debriefing will provide interest, stimulation and relaxation – an interesting but not impossible combination.

The use of closed circuit television

Sooner or later most role-play tutors will want to consider the use of closed circuit television (CCTV) to record and play back the enactment. We must therefore look at the way in which this might be done, and at the advantages and disadvantages. We could have considered this at almost any point in the book, but it has been put in this chapter because in practice it is the debriefing that CCTV affects most.

There are obvious advantages in obtaining a record of what went on in the course of a role-play. Players may be reminded of the sequence of events, the detail of what was said, who said what, and the way they said it. An objective record can resolve disputes and enable students to study their own performances.

Many of these facilities are provided by a sound recording which is much simpler and cheaper to obtain than a video recording. Why then go to all the extra trouble and expense? The answer is that the sound recording can capture the intonation of the voice but not gestures and facial expression. People are becoming more and more aware that a great deal of information is transmitted by non-verbal means and only a visual medium, therefore, can truly capture this information. It is also very difficult to identify individual speakers on an audio tape, particularly where they are overlapping and interrupting one another.

Television can amplify subtle non-verbal cues and enable students to see their importance in communication. It also gives the participants an opportunity to see the interaction as a whole and not just from one point of view. Its major disadvantage, apart from the extra work it entails, is that it is liable to slow down the debriefing unless carefully controlled. On the other hand it can introduce some order and structure into this process if required.

Other uses

It is worth noting that the use of CCTV for getting a record of the session is not its only application in role-play. One of the most interesting ways of using it is for the transmission of information within the role-play itself. We have already seen the problems of incorporating too much information in the writing of role-briefs. This can be partly overcome by feeding in extra information during the role-play. But there are obvious problems about delivering a lot of extra information by the printed word. An effective alternative is to incorporate it in a television transmission under the guise of a news bulletin or pre-recorded interview. It could even be used as a means of transmitting information from one room to another in the case of a role-play of a union-management dispute, for example.

Another use of CCTV is for a later evaluation of the role-play. This may take different forms. It may be that the tutor wishes to analyse the time spent on different phases of the interaction or some other aspect of the exercise which would indicate to him how the learning process went. This could be particularly useful if the debriefing itself was also recorded. Again the fact that the recording can be played repeatedly means that different observers can analyse their reactions to it independently and can carry out separate ratings for subsequent comparison. This not only provides a means of considering the role-play, but also offers an opportunity to train and compare observers.

The main use to which CCTV is likely to be put, however, is as an aid to debriefing, and the remainder of this chapter is devoted to exploring this application. Although there are advantages in the use of television facilities there are also disadvantages and dangers; attention will be drawn to these as the techniques themselves are described.

Making a recording

The basic problem of using a film or video camera is that the angle of vision for normal lenses is limited. The depth of focus under average lighting conditions is also limited. This means that the maximum number of people who can be kept in clear focus at any one time is five or six, certainly not more than eight. For larger groups, or where the participants are not static and cannot be positioned for the convenience of the operator, either several cameras must be used or a single, very mobile one.

There are essentially three ways in which a CCTV recording can be made:

- using remote controlled cameras;
- using a studio with tripod cameras;
- using a small hand-held camera.

The use of remote controlled cameras (with a one-way screen for the operator) implies fixed positions for the cameras. This means that several cameras are needed to cover the field from a number of different angles, and that either the operator has to be extremely dexterous in panning, tilting and cutting from one camera to another, or that more than one operator has to be used. There are, however, some types of situation, a face-to-face interview between two seated people for example, in which this set-up is useful although expensive.

The full studio set-up is considerably more expensive of course, but the greater objection to studios is their artificiality and the tension they can create. It is difficult to get students to relax in a high-ceilinged room bristling with lights, equipment and people. Moreover the acoustics of such spaces, whilst ideal for the microphone, are often most unsuitable for people holding normal conversations and the lighting, again ideal for the camera, is unsuitable for creating the required atmosphere.

Whilst some trainers and teachers may make use of more sophisticated equipment, the majority plump for the simple hand-held camera on the grounds of cheapness, ease of control and simplicity of use. With the cost of home video equipment dropping all the time it puts the use of CCTV within reach of everyone.

The disadvantages of the one-camera set-up are:

- loss of technical quality;
- bias introduced by choice of camera angle;
- intrusion of the camera;
- wear and tear on the operator.

These disadvantages are more notional than real. As long as the recording is regarded as an *aide-memoire* rather than as a product of the entertainment industry, its technical quality should take a lower priority than such things as ease of use and general compatibility.

Bias is an inevitable part of any process which only records a part and not the whole; it is impossible to avoid in the observation of human interactions because they are so complex.

In the case of multi-camera installations editing takes the form of the choice of camera positions and which particular view to record at any particular moment. In the case of the single camera it lies with the choices made by the cameraman.. Where the operator is also the tutor, however, this handicap can be turned into an advantage by using the camera deliberately to emphasize and comment upon those aspects to which the tutor wishes to draw attention. In this event there should be little need for further comment from him during the debriefing; the pictures speak for themselves, and the discussion can be left largely to the students.

Many people using CCTV for the first time are concerned that the presence of the camera will influence the behaviour of the participants. They therefore go to great lengths to conceal the camera or minimize its effects. In practice it will be found that after an initial period of a few minutes the participants become oblivious to the camera even where the operator is walking around with it. They will adapt to it – provided that the role-play itself is sufficiently motivating.

! WARNING !

Don't forget that the playback of a recording will take several times the length of the recording itself.

When videoing a role-play session it is worth starting the recording a few moments before the 'official' start of the session and even more important to continue the recording for a few moments after the end. These transition points between 'reality' and 'role-play' can yield valuable insights into the attitudes and behaviour of the students. They are points of uncertainty when students are searching for a framework into which they can fit, and their comments may sometimes reveal the problem which is preventing their role-play from being fully effective.

Another point of importance at the beginning of a recording is to remember to make a note of the number on the tape-counter. Ideally one should make a note of the number on the counter as each critical incident occurs so that it is possible to find the place on the tape quickly during the debriefing session. Often this is difficult or impossible, in which case a useful tip is to make a note of the counter readings at the beginning and end of the session. If the tutor then makes a physical or mental note of the times at which various interesting events occurred, it should be possible to estimate the correct counter number by interpolation. Thus, if a total of 400 counter units was recorded in a session lasting 12 minutes then the counter number after three minutes will be one quarter of the way through, ie 100. After eight minutes it will be two-thirds of the way, ie counter number 266, and so on.

Replaying the recording

Video-recording is a powerful technique and the sight of oneself on television for the first time is usually somewhat daunting. Role-players are likely to feel sensitive to criticism even without the cold penetration of the TV camera, and the approach to debriefing should therefore be even more sensitive than usual when using CCTV.

The role-players should always be asked for their own reactions to the exercise before the tape is replayed. In the first place this allows them to voice criticism of themselves before they become defensive. Usually people are more critical of their own performance than others, and whatever is revealed by the videotape is likely to be less disparaging than their own self-evaluation. Second, their comments provide some sort of a baseline from which they can judge the comments on how the others saw them. Lastly, it is useful to obtain the players' subjective reactions and feelings immediately after the action has finished and before they settle down to a lengthy period of analysis.

It is also useful at this stage to sound out the participants on how they think an 'ideal' interview, or whatever, would have gone. This provides a reference point against which the actual interaction can be evaluated.

The normal procedure when playing the recording is to allow it to proceed until someone wants it stopped in order to make a comment. That person can be the tutor or a player or observer, and it is important to ensure that students feel able to ask for the tape to be stopped if they want. It has already been pointed out that the first part of a debriefing session should enable students to express themselves freely; any feeling that the playback of the recording is being controlled by the tutor will nullify this aspect of the debriefing.

HINT Stop the tape early on to set a precedent of stopping the tape whenever a participant wants to.

When someone asks for the tape to be stopped and there is a discussion about what was going on, the tutor can encourage the group to aim its criticism and comment towards the screen. Commentators should be encouraged to voice their opinions in terms such as: 'The chairman interrupted too soon there', 'The clerk on the left could have shown the applicant the form', 'When she turned round they should have realized what the problem was'. In this way the comments are depersonalized and are seen to be comments about the way in which the roles interacted rather than criticism of the players themselves.

TIP Try stopping the tape and asking what happened next – it demonstrates the need for cross-checking one's memory of events.

The temptation to hang too much on to the analysis of a few seconds' material must be avoided. We have all found ourselves at one time or another starting to concentrate on more and more detail in a recording. Once one starts to ask about a facial expression or arm movement, once attention is drawn to particular words or intonations, then it is possible to question every gesture, every syllable. Much of this is legitimate and indeed represents the pay-off for all the trouble of making the videorecording. But there is an appropriate level of detail for everything and the tutor must be on guard not to run an analysis into the ground with detailed observation. The best way to avoid this is always to keep firmly in one's mind the idea that the CCTV recording should be used as a notebook and stimulus to discussion, not as a microscope.

There is another minor but irritating aspect of CCTV playback which should be mentioned and that is the stop-frame facility which is available on most videorecorders. It is natural for the tutor to use this when stopping the action, and to leave a still frame on the screen whilst commenting on the scene. There are two objections to leaving this image on the screen for an extended period. The first is a technical one; on the cheaper recorders there is a danger that the tape will be worn by being held in a stationary position against the play-back head. This will result in a momentary blank spot on the tape. The second problem is that any image of a person, particularly a facial image, held stationary in mid-movement for a long time begins to look ridiculous. This is unfair on the role-player, and will distract from the more serious job in hand. If the discussion starts to extend longer than the tutor at first intended, it is a good idea to stop the recorder in the normal way rather than leave it on stop-frame.

! WARNING !

Try not to use stop-frame. Use the normal stop instead.

Drawbacks

Apart from the problems which can occur when using CCTV, there are also one or two drawbacks which arise from the nature of the medium itself. Because it appears to encapsulate all the essentials of the role-play session, it is tempting to use it for viewing at other times away from the original group. There is nothing wrong in this of course, provided that it was made clear to the role-players that the videorecording might be used for demonstration purposes at a later date. The danger arises where there is a lack of shared convention between the original players and the viewers. Unless there is time to discuss the recording with one of the original group, the viewer can easily interpret responses in a different way to the role-players who are in the scene. This in turn means that they will misunderstand the reasons for the players' behaviour.

The use of CCTV also tends to delay the immediacy of feedback. The closer the feedback can be to the original action the more effective it will be. The use of CCTV, however well conducted, is liable to introduce delays and extend the time taken to cover all the points.

This in turn leads on to a further aspect, the temptation to use the recording just because it is there. Television is only part of the total teaching resource. Like any other resource it is there to be used at the right time, the right place and when it is appropriate to the teaching that is being done.

! WARNING !

If the playback isn't necessary – don't use it.

If the discussion and analysis during the debriefing take on a life of their own, tutors should be grateful for their good fortune and not tempt providence by insisting on playing back bits of the recording over which they have sweated and toiled. It may be all right to climb mountains just because they are there; the same philosophy does not apply to video recordings. This temptation becomes almost imperative where elaborate studio facilities have been used. Not only is there pressure from the technical staff for a sign that their efforts have not all been in vain, but the students themselves will want to see the results of all that organization, whether or not it has any educational or training value.

> Youth and community
> Communication
> Teaching
> Interviewing
> Committees
> Group dynamics
> Psychiatric nursing
> Counselling
> Sales training

Figure 8.7 Areas of use with CCTV

Using CCTV wisely

The use of closed circuit television grafts one powerful tool (CCTV) on to another (role-play). This combined force can reveal a great deal about individual students, their attitudes and behaviour. As with any other powerful tool this combination can be used constructively or destructively. The students may acquire more confidence and strength by being shown ways of improving their skills and by being given insights into behavioural situations, or they may be shown up as being inadequate or ineffectual. The difference lies in the sensitivity and self-discipline of the tutor. Above all, the technique should only be used where the tutor is confident that he has a warm and receptive group which will be helpful and positive in its approach to its members. In allocating time to view the recording, the tutor should make sure that there is time allowed at the end to talk out problems and possibly to rehearse difficult points again.

Not all role-plays are suitable for videorecording. The benefits are greatest where there is an interpersonal exchange involving non-verbal as well as verbal skills. Figure 8.7 gives a list of some of the areas which are particularly suited for use with CCTV.

9 *Further aspects of role-play*

Other ways of using role-play

So far we have looked at what might be regarded as the more conventional and common uses of role-play. These can be grouped under the following headings:

- Arousing interest, providing motivation.
- Exploring subjects.
- Teaching skills, developing communication.
- Testing alternative behaviour.
- Changing attitudes.
- Helping with personal conflicts and problems.

Any categorization is arbitrary to some extent: there are bound to be overlaps between areas, and many role-plays fulfil a number of functions. There are, however, a number of other uses to which role-play can be put which have not been mentioned before, or only in passing. The remainder of this chapter will be devoted to enumerating these areas and discussing some of them in greater detail.

Modelling

There are some teaching tasks where it is convenient to have a model or dummy on which the students can practise. In the case of medical students these are called surrogates or simulated patients (although the latter term is also used to indicate manufactured or computer models) and the simulator or role-player is carefully trained to respond to a medical examination in exactly the same way as with a real patient. This technique is used widely in medical schools, particularly in North America. The same technique can be used for training in first-aid and nursing, and a flourishing organization in the UK, the Casualties Union, which was formed as part of the Civil Defence in 1942, now has branches in Australia and South Africa in addition to its 30 branches in the UK. Its members are assessed for their ability to portray not only the symptoms of a sick or injured person, but also the way in which these change according to the handling and treatment received.

The advantages of using simulated patients can be summarized as follows.

● Avoids tiring, embarrassing or hurting patients.
● Allows repetitive examination, thus giving each student the same experience.
● Enables the tutor to stop and start at will.
● Frees real patients for use in more advanced teaching.
● Gives greater control over the situation.
● Gives the student feedback from the 'patient'.

Another quite different use of modelling is in the training of observers for sociological or psychological research, or indeed for any other observational purpose. Here the problem is to train the person to discriminate between different types of behaviour or different elements of a piece of complex behaviour such as a skill. The model or dummy is asked to perform certain actions whilst the observers note down their observations. Here again it is possible to observe real life activities, but the use of a simulated situation gives the trainer more control and flexibility.

Specific training

Role-play techniques can be used in a variety of training situations, some of which are of special importance or interest.

Listening skills

There is considerable use of role-play as a training technique in the training of counsellors of all types. Typical groups which use it are

Relate and the Samaritans. The problem that it poses, however, is that it is a technique which tends to put a premium on verbal skills and, when used in this context, it is not always easy to demonstrate that silence and atmosphere are as important as words. The required results can only be achieved if the simulated client can provide sensitive and accurate feedback which discriminates between good and bad use of talking.

Assertion

There has been an enormous expansion in the number of courses on assertion training. This has arisen because of an increased aware-ness that individuals have a right to assert themselves and that assertion is not the same as aggression, in fact aggression can actu-ally be counterproductive.

Role-play is almost tailor-made for assertion training. It is possi-ble to construct a series of carefully graded exercises which take students from their present position to the ultimate goal of self-confidence in whatever situation they themselves may want to define. This may be the ability to take back faulty goods to a shop, ask the boss for a rise, or just take part in group discussions. The ultimate objectives rest with the student; the trainer can provide a series of structured experiences which lead up to them.

A new use which is developing for role-play is training to deal with threats of violence. The technique, which is essentially one of defusing the situation, lends itself to demonstration and rehearsal by means of role-play.

Empathy training

This is a process which is not widely used at present but which has great potential. There are many jobs in which professionals such as teachers or social workers are dealing with clients who are disadvan-taged in some way. It is difficult for them to know what it is like to be disabled but role-play methods have been devised which mimic the problems which the disabled have to face. At a simple level it is possi-ble to blindfold someone and ask them to role-play a blind person in a particular situation; more complex arrangements can imitate the problems of the physically handicapped or the person who suffers from dyslexia. There are also simulations involving role-play which highlight the problems of the financially disadvantaged.

The advantage of this type of training is that it enables the stu-dent to perceive clearly the effects of the outside world on the disadvantaged. After having been put in their shoes for a while it is easier for the professional to make the right decisions in the future when dealing with this type of case.

Desensitization

Just as it is possible to train clients to assert themselves more vigorously, so is it possible to desensitize them to traumatic experiences. Repeated re-enactments of an anxiety-provoking situation in a supportive setting can reduce the avoidance response. For example, one can prepare students for taking an examination or for dealing with emergency situations such as fire or accidents. The technique is to set up a simulated situation which is then repeatedly enacted, possibly in a more and more severe or threatening form, so that the student gradually becomes desensitized to the situation.

Assessment

The use of simulations and role-play as a form of assessment is well established. Beginning with the Prussian army at the turn of the century, and developed to a fine art by the British army during the Second World War, the idea is simply to place the candidate in a situation as close as possible to the type of situation in which his abilities will be needed in real life. Thus exercises have been developed around such things as the problem of getting across a river with a minimum amount of equipment.

Although physical activity was associated with these tests, the important aspects which were observed by the trainers were related much more to decision-making, working as a group, leadership, flexibility and so on. It is only a short step to realize that a lot of the physical accoutrements were unnecessary and that a large proportion of the assessment could be carried out by role-playing the situation in the classroom. From there it is a short step to apply the same methods to the assessment of industrial and business managers.

In the United States the use of Assessment Centres for the selection of potential staff for key posts is well established. It is an expensive business, but not half as costly as making the wrong choice of manager for a senior post. In the UK the Civil Service Selection Board has been using group role-play as an assessment technique for many years. The classical exercise consists of a group of five candidates who are given a series of complex interlinking problems. Each candidate has to chair the group for 15 minutes during which the group seeks to analyse his problem and come to a conclusion. The group is observed by a senior civil servant, a psychologist and a young administrator who are looking for the generation of ideas, analytical capacity and interpersonal skills.

A more structured use of role-play as an assessment technique is possible. Suppose that it is desired to test student nurses on the correct procedures to follow when first interviewing a psychiatric patient. A role-play can be set up in which the nurse is asked to do precisely that, but with a surrogate patient. The trainer observes the interaction and scores the nurse's actions against a prepared list of what should be done. In principle, any scenario which is used for teaching purposes can also be used for assessment purposes. This is particularly the case in jobs such as marriage guidance counselling where role-play and similar activities form a major part of the training procedure. In these cases a similar group of role-plays can be used in the initial stages to assess the suitability of candidates.

The basis of using role-play as an assessment technique is to observe the candidate's behaviour in a realistic simulation of part of the job they may have to do. This makes it possible to assess the performance of a wide variety of workers from managers to shop-floor personnel in situations where they have to interact with other people.

There has grown up around this area the idea that role-play is widely used to put people under artificial stress in order to test out their behaviour under extreme conditions. Little evidence of this has come to the author's notice, although it may well be used in the training of secret service agents. In spite of the lack of evidence, however, it is one of the principal reasons why students tend to regard roleplaying exercises with suspicion. It is time that this particular story was knocked on the head as a fantasy in the minds of trainers and trainees. Grilling under a bright light belongs exclusively to the realm of adventure stories.

Simulated cases

The use of case studies is well established in the teaching of business management. Some courses are entirely based on the case study method. Usually the presentation of the case to be considered is done by means of a written description. The students then consider the problem either singly or in groups and present their answers in the same form as the case was itself presented, ie on paper, or by a verbal presentation. The tutor analyses their responses and points out things that they have missed or the conflicting aspects of the case.

Role-play may be used to advantage both in the presentation of the problem and the solutions. It may be in the form of short excerpts on film or video, enacted by professional actors or by students. These short scenes can give a vivid impression of the background to a problem or of the problem itself. There is also the possibility of playing out scenes from the case in front of the class.

The same possibilities exist for solutions with the advantage of a live enactment that it can be amended and replayed at will according to the ideas put forward by the class. The use of these techniques can enliven the routine presentation of case studies and also lead to the more active use of role-play as described in the earlier parts of this book. It falls into the first functional type of role-play categorized in Figure 4.1, the 'Describe' category.

Research

In the same way that role-play enables students to experiment with their behaviour without undue expense and danger, so is it possible for the social scientist to set up experimental situations for investigation. One of the best known examples of this technique was the Stanford Prison Experiment in the United States. In the summer of 1971 a mock prison was constructed in the basement of the psychology building at Stanford University. A group of volunteers was split at random into prisoners and guards. The idea was to play the simulation for two weeks and to study the way in which the relationship between the two groups developed.

The outcome of the study was dramatic. The volunteers entered so much into their allocated roles that they began to show signs of changing personality; those playing the parts of prisoners became mostly passive and docile, suffering from an acute loss of contact with reality. Because of this the experimenters terminated the study at the end of the sixth day (Haney, Banks and Zimbardo, 1973).

This illustrates the way in which role-players enter easily into their role, and gives added support to the argument that it can be almost as valid to study people playing a role as it is to study the actual real life situation. This opens the door to the possibility of transferring the more difficult or dangerous experiments, such as the Milgram electric shock experiments, to a role-played environment. The whole question is discussed by Cohen and Manion (1980) in Chapter 12 of their book.

There are other ways in which role-play may be used in problem-solving or research. It can be used as a predictive tool by setting up international crisis simulations and playing them through with knowledgeable people. Not only can the outcome of the simulation be used to predict the possible outcome of a similar crisis in the real world, but the simulation can be repeated with different variables. In some of the accounts of these international crisis simulations it is remarked how unnervingly close the conclusions are to subsequent events.

As indicated at the beginning of this book, the whole subject of role is one to which social scientists and sociologists attach considerable importance. It is easy to see that role-play could be used to explore some aspects of role itself and especially such concepts as 'role-conflict', 'role-overload', 'role-deviancy' or even the idea of self' as a cultural product. Moreover, the use of role-play may throw light on cultural differences in behaviour; one could imagine setting up a simple role-play scene and asking people of different cultural backgrounds to play the same part in the scene, thus revealing the different approaches to the same task. This could easily be extended to the study of linguistic differences.

Change agent

Change can be thought of as a process which normally goes through three stages. The first stage is to unfreeze, to loosen up the existing state; the second is to rearrange the parts into a different pattern; the third is to refreeze or consolidate the new pattern. These steps follow closely the workings of a role-play with its warm-up, enactment, debriefing and follow-up. Role-play falls naturally into the function of change agent. How can this be used in practice?

The trainer can get a good response by working with a group of people who normally work together. After introductory warm-up activities, which include discussions of their most pressing problems, these problems are converted into a role-play scenario which is used to explore possible solutions. The debriefing and follow-up will include a discussion of the way in which the new methods can be integrated into the existing system.

Role-play may also be used in a more direct way to change certain aspects of people's personality and behaviour where this is desired by the clients themselves. As with hypnotism, the change comes about through the desire and effort of the subject; it cannot be imposed from outside. One of the most promising uses is in developing greater spontaneity. It is one of the problems of our culture that spontaneity is suppressed in us during our early years and we find it difficult to regain this enthusiastic independence. Creative drama is one road to regaining this spirit; the more structured role-play aimed at specific circumstances is another.

Revision

Most readers would agree that revision is one of the most boring and depressing activities which a student has to undertake. The whole concept of going through material which has already been studied carries with it the seeds of disenchantment. For the good student there is the tedium of repeating 90 per cent of the material that he already knows and understands; for the less able student there is the frustration of going through the material which he did not understand in the first place.

Since one of the most powerful aspects of role-play is its ability to involve and motivate, it is likely to be a good medium for revision exercises. These can take the form of problem situations to which the student has to respond. The same situations can be used for both teaching and revision; this has the added attraction of providing a familiar background for the student to remember by. Revision can be made even more enjoyable and memorable if the role-play contains a competitive element in it like a game.

Learning by writing

Creating a role-play is fun. It enables even the shyest and most retiring person to indulge in a little creativity. There is the possibility of making new micro-worlds within which the writer can create conflict and give birth to extra characters at will.

Creating a role-play is also hard work. It involves gaining an understanding of the problem and how it relates to surrounding circumstances. It necessitates checking on facts and figures and a lot of deep thinking about the consequences of various actions. To successfully create a role-play one must already have a thorough understanding of the subject and the characters involved.

The result is that writing a role-play exercise is both fun and educational. One of the best ways to learn a subject is to teach it but teaching involves all sorts of other skills which the student may not have, such as the ability to stand in front of the class and talk, or the ability to maintain discipline. Writing a role-play does not involve any of these skills. It does not, in the first instance anyway, even require a particularly good writing style or an ability to use words in a sophisticated way.

Writing a role-play means the ability to manipulate ideas about the interaction of people with each other and their environment. A certain natural empathy with others is helpful, as is a flexible imagination. The main task is to gather information and to put it together in a meaningful way in relation to the characters who are going to people the exercise. There is ample scope for researching material and discussing the impact of decisions and behaviour in the particular surroundings which the writer has decided to create.

A technique which is well worth exploring is that of getting one group of students to prepare a role-play for another group. Group A, for example, may arrange a role-play where members of group B play the parts of a management team who have to bring in some new methods of working. The members of group A, who have written the scenario and role-briefs, play the parts of the workers, shop-stewards etc. While group A have been preparing their role-play, group B will have been similarly engaged on another scenario and the two role-plays can be enacted in succession. This is an excellent way of encouraging the less enthusiastic learner to become involved.

Other experiential methods

One of the difficulties experienced by those who are interested in the use of role-play as a teaching method is that it belongs to a much wider group of procedures which can collectively be thought of as experiential techniques. (That is to say they rely for their effect on the student's actual experience of emotions, feelings, communications, situations and other intangibles.) The reason for this difficulty is that there are similarities between the techniques which certainly cause the layman to confuse them and sometimes cause confusion even among the practitioners themselves. This chapter attempts to clarify some of the distinctions and to place role-play within the context of the other methods.

Figure 9.1 is a map of the territory which has been designed to show the relationships between the various components; those paths which lead towards role-play are indicated by the boxed headings. The next section discusses the relationship between these activities and is followed by a more detailed description of some of the more important areas relevant to role-play.

Looking at oneself

Although the field of educational simulation is a broad one which encompasses or overlaps with models, simulators and games, there is a clear-cut boundary between those which entail some form of enactment and those which do not. Where the students are involved in a form of enactment, their interests can be divided into those that concern them personally and those that concern others. Taking the area to the left of the diagram which concerns the student, they may be encouraged to explore their behaviour and feelings in a non-directive, unstructured way such as is done in a T-group where the facilitator's role is to allow a session to develop under the pressure of its own dynamic or motive force. Alternatively, as indicated by the right-hand branch, the session may be more structured, using exercises to make students more aware of their attitudes, behaviour and feelings.

The outcome of these structured experiences is to enable the student to change. The characteristic transformation will be towards feelings, attitudes and behaviours which are more acceptable, but it raises the key question – acceptable to whom? Broadly speaking one might say that the student will function better in society, but this can cover a variety of matters. He may become better in selling refrigerators or some other aspect of his job; he may learn how to cope with social interactions such as buying a rail ticket or ordering a meal; he may become less violent in his reactions to stress; he may just feel better in himself. Acquiring some of these skills or attitudes would be classed as therapy if the subject was a patient in a mental hospital, education if a child at school, and training if an employee at work. The distinctions are not all that clear.

In practice the intention behind the teaching on the one hand and the severity of the student's maladjustment on the other permits

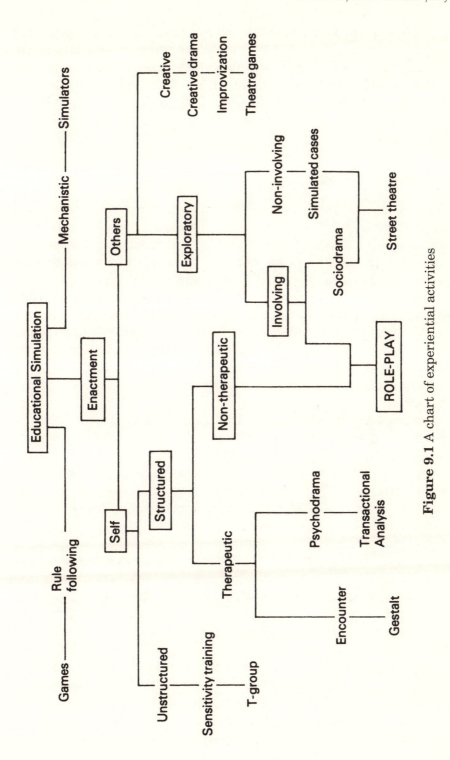

Figure 9.1 A chart of experiential activities

the division (shown in Figure 9. 1) into structured exercises which are therapeutic and non-therapeutic. The therapeutic activities are intended for those people who have expressed a wish to become better adjusted and comfortable within their society, or for those for whom this need has been identified by professional workers. Even here, however, one can see the difficulty in making absolute distinctions.

Looking at others

Turning now to the other major division on the right of the diagram, there is an equally complex series of activities concerned with the behaviour of others. These activities are divided for the purposes of this book into two streams: the exploratory and the creative. On the creative side there is the highly successful use of drama in schools as one of the creative media in which children can fabricate their own imaginative world using such approaches as improvization and theatre games. On the exploratory side there are methods such as the use of simulated cases, including filmed examples and specially prepared actors, where the learning is vicarious and the simulation itself does not involve the student except as a spectator.

On the other hand there are exploratory methods which involve the student, and these can themselves follow one of two directions, either towards the analysis of behaviours found in individuals or towards an analysis of social groups, ie nurses, families, immigrants, teachers. The former activity is what we have been calling role-play; the latter is an activity more commonly known as sociodrama.

As seen in Figure 9. 1, there is a link between sociodrama, simulated cases, and street theatre. Street theatre is an interesting phenomenon which incorporates aspects of many other social and political activities. In terms of this book it is a technique which uses theatrical improvisation to involve the audience in an exploration of society and social groups. Hence its appearance as part of the chart.

The methods which are sometimes associated in a general way with role-play are psychodrama, fixed role therapy, sociodrama, encounter groups, simulated cases and creative drama. These are discussed individually below.

Psychodrama

The origins of psychodrama stem from the seminal work of J L Moreno who is also credited with the development of sociometry, group psychotherapy and sociodrama. Moreno was interested in the problems of interpersonal relationships and the application of play, encounter and theatrical techniques to their solution. In the 1920s he founded a 'theatre of spontaneity' in which issues dealing with current events were dramatized, but later he became interested in the application of the theatrical setting to the treatment of individuals, marriage relationships and small groups.

One of the periods in his life which stimulated his thinking was when he was carrying out research into training schools for delinquent girls. He argued that there was a need to provide them with wider experiences to prepare them for life outside the institution and instigated a type of social skills role-play with an emphasis on personal exploration. During the development of his ideas he used many terms such as 'encounter' and 'here-and-now' which have become popular in the human potential movement of today.

The classic psychodrama stage is an area consisting of three levels with shallow steps between which the players can move up and down. These levels sometimes symbolize the degree to which the player has entered into the role; sometimes they symbolize the depth of emotional involvement and penetration into the subconscious.

As with role-play, the first phase is the warm-up. The emphasis during this period is to get the players to relax and lose some of their inhibitions. One of the most important aspects of this warm-up period is the identification of a personal problem belonging to one of the group, or a problem which is common to the group members.

The director (psychodrama uses this term to denote the therapist) then brings the protagonist to the stage and discusses the problem briefly in order to redefine it in terms of a concrete example which can be enacted. The protagonist describes the scene together with the other characters; members of the group are then brought forward to play those parts. These other people are called auxiliary egos, or sometimes just auxiliaries. The protagonist teaches them their parts by briefly portraying each of the other figures in his drama. Throughout the enactment there is interchange between the protagonist and the group so that the other players get closer and closer to playing the real characters which the protagonist deals with in real life.

Once the enactment has begun the director uses all the techniques which were described in Chapter 7 such as role-reversal, mirroring, doubling, chair and silent auxiliary, together with other techniques using fantasy, symbolism and confrontation. The aim is to help the protagonist identify emotional blocks. During the enactment the director encourages the protagonist to go from peripheral to central issues and to reach a point of emotional openness or catharsis. When this has been reached the third, constructive stage begins.

This stage of the psychodrama is one of working through. The protagonist uses group support to deal with issues of 're-entry' into the outside world. These items are dealt with respectively by behavioural practice – similar to skills training in role-play; sharing – a process familiar to those who use any of the group therapies; and closing – a mixture of summarizing, planning and finishing rituals.

This account of psychodramatic techniques should suffice to illustrate the close parallel between psychodrama and role-play. This has sometimes led to a confusion between the two techniques and consequently to a blurring of objectives. Provided the tutor is clear in his own mind about the purpose of role-play within his own teaching programme, there can only be advantage to be gained in a cross-fertilization between the two fields. Those readers who wish to follow up this brief account are referred to the eminently readable book by Blatner (1973).

Fixed role therapy

A more recent derivation of psychodrama which stems from George A Kelly's personal construct theory, is fixed role therapy. The key to an understanding of this is the idea of role being an activity which is carried out in the light of one's understanding of how other people view it. Thus the emphasis is on other people's points of view as defining the way one responds.

In fixed role therapy clients write a character sketch of themselves from the perspective of another who knows them intimately. An enactment sketch (similar to a role-brief) is prepared which purposely experiments with an unusual dimension, eg a cautious client may be asked to enact an assertive role. The client then acts 'in role' for two weeks, say, and during therapy sessions the therapist treats them as if they really were the other modified character.

As with role-play, there is no threat to the integrity of the client's original personality because they are only playing a hypothetical character; they are experimenting with a new dimension. It has been shown that on the whole this type of structured experience is less threatening and dangerous than the completely unstructured approaches which are used in other therapies; the ability to 'hide behind' the role as an ultimate resort can be very useful. Nevertheless, this acting of a role is a powerful mechanism for change. It is actually all the more powerful in the case of clients who find it difficult to act the part since, unlike the more skilled actor, they have to invest more of themselves into the part in order to make anything of it.

During the therapeutic sessions the therapist may use any of the techniques we have discussed to help the client's understanding of the other's point of view.

Sociodrama

The previous two techniques have been ones used to explore and alleviate individual problems. Sociodrama is a technique used to explore the problems posed by social groupings. Although it has been given a special name it is identical in most ways to the use of role-play in groups whose aims are to learn about social problems and the behaviour of social groups. A typical problem might be the inter-racial stress in inner cities, and in particular the way in which the police relate to minority groups. This could be a subject which arises in such diverse circumstances as self-awareness groups within the black community, community policing courses, or in a social sciences course at school or college.

The procedure would be to draw out the critical aspects of the problem from the students and to construct, with their help, a scenario which illustrates one concrete example. Players would then be chosen to enact the scene and they would be asked to report their feelings and attitudes during the debriefing stage. This leads on to further discussion of the problem, further refinement and definition, and to a further example or variation of the first one. The process continues for as long as is required.

The emphasis in sociodrama is on the problems associated with the social role which an actor is playing rather than on the individual's problems. Its aim is to clarify rather than cure, but within this limitation it is a lively way of stimulating interest in global issues and can be used in a variety of contexts.

Encounter group

It may seem strange to include encounter groups in a book on role-play. It is true that encounter groups, gestalt therapy and many other experiential therapies belong to a rather different realm from that of traditional role-play. The activities in this realm tend to have certain external characteristics in common. They consist of small groups (from eight to 18 members) that are relatively unstructured but have a facilitator who helps the group members to express their feelings and thoughts. The group strives towards an atmosphere of mutual trust within which group members can give each other immediate feedback on the effect of their behaviour on other members of the group. Depending on the structure of the group and the particular type of activity, the facilitator may endeavour to remove some of the inhibitions which govern normal social contact in order to facilitate change within the group and its members.

The exercises and activities which are used within encounter groups are sufficiently diverse to provide for a range of needs within the group. Many of them are aimed at stimulating the imagination, enabling members to focus on feelings, relax, or become aware of themselves. One cluster of exercises uses the same format as role-playing, that is to say one of the group acts out a role suggested by the facilitator. The purpose, however, will be to confront personal problems or inhibitions. They may be asked to act 'as if you were. . . ' in order to bring hidden emotions to the surface. The roles therefore will be that of themselves when a child, or as a parent or a loved one. The aim is for catharsis and emotional release.

It follows that one of the most important adjuncts to encounter group work is the support which is available to group members after the event. If people are to be encouraged to lower their defences and expose themselves and their frailties then the facilitator must be willing and able to give them the necessary support for as long as it is needed. Although many tutors who use role-play in a sensitive way may be technically competent to run an encounter group, they must first ensure that they have searched into their own egos sufficiently to be aware of their own motivations and weaknesses. They must then ensure that they are competent and able to provide ongoing support to anyone who may have uncovered things during the group-work which have left them feeling exposed.

Creative drama

Just as there is a distinction between role-play and theatrical acting, so is there one between role-play and creative drama. As with
some of the other cases we have looked at in this chapter, the distinction is more one of purpose than technique.

The objectives of creative drama are the same as those of the
other subjects grouped under the heading of the expressive arts,
namely to enable students to express themselves using body, voice
and instruments. It is a mixture of loosening up, teaching of skills,
and stimulation of the imagination. It results in the development of
more self-confidence, a release of innate creativity, and an
increased awareness of the value of the arts in general.

The casual visitor looking at creative drama sessions from the
outside could well mistake them for a role-play simulation in progress. A close inspection, however, would show that the emphasis is
on free expression and not so much on a constrained situation. Most
importantly there is no question of checking the validity of actions
against real life, or an analysis afterwards of how the situation
might have been handled differently. The enjoyment evolves within
the creative drama itself not from an analysis or playback afterwards.

The activities described above are some of the methods which are
occasionally confused with role-play, or whose ambits overlap it.
Tutors who are interested and want to develop their techniques as
far as they will go will learn a lot from some of these areas. They
have a common theme of using the imagination of the student to
create a world from which one can learn.

10 Computers and the Internet

Since the essence of role-play is the two-way communication between people, it is natural to ask whether there are other means of communication that could be used as a basis for the exercise. There have been isolated instances of using portable telephone exchanges to provide telephone links in business simulation games, and it would also be possible to use a video link to role-play across distances, but the desk-top computer and the establishment of the Internet have brought potentially powerful tools which could be used to develop new types of role-play.

Computer Moderated Communication (CMC)

Computers can be used to store and manipulate data, including text-based information and graphic displays. It is therefore possible to use them to store and display reference material or to feed information into the role-play at pre-determined times.

Consider, for example, a role-play involving a production manager discussing production targets with a line foreman. The manager, or indeed both players, can have all the details of production available to them without having to refer to reams of paperwork. Not only that, but they can use the computer to manipulate the figures across different production lines to see the effect of changes. Similarly in the role-play of a social worker or benefits officer interviewing a client, the text of the rules and guidelines issued by the government can be stored and readily available.

A major advantage of using the computer in this way is that it will reduce the scope for wild invention on the part of the players (see Chapter 7) by defining more closely the parameters of the role-play. This does not mean that participants will be inhibited from genuine creative ideas, but the tutor can more readily circumscribe those areas where information and guidelines are available and mandatory. This can still leave large areas available for creative invention.

Mention has been made of using newspapers or photographs to give information within the role-play; this may also be done by using the computer as a display device and issuing the text of news bulletins, etc. An example of this might be the use of presentation software such as Powerpoint to display a sequence of news items in a role-play that involves a developing scenario.

All of these uses, however, are only using the computer as a tool to mimic existing communication methods. In many cases the computer is merely taking the administrative burden from the tutor. Now that we have the ability to connect up computers into complex networks via the Internet a whole new range of possibilities opens out. The remainder of this chapter explores some of those possibilities.

The Internet

The Internet is a highly complex system based on 'service providers', which are linked into a network by means of telephone lines, fibre optic cable, and satellite. These 'service providers' are large computers which run 24 hours a day. They are usually accessed by individuals via a local dial-up telephone line. There are other components of the Internet, but it is the service providers that act as the main interface between the individual and the network itself. The Internet environment is sometimes referred to in more fanciful terms as 'cyberspace'.

There are a number of services that use the Internet as a platform for distribution. Those which are of main interest here are:

- email;
- mailing lists;
- conferences;
- usenet news groups;

- bulletin boards;
- Internet relay chat;
- MUDs and MOOs;
- World Wide Web (WWW).

Email

Most professional people will be aware of, or indeed users of, email by now. It is possible to send text from one person to another very quickly. The sender sends a message to their service provider, which then sends it on to the service provider of the recipient. The message is stored there until the recipient connects to their service provider, and the message is then downloaded to their personal computer.

This opens out the possibility of a 'conversation' between two or (by means of copying) more role-players anywhere in the world. The 'conversation' is of course text based, and is asynchronous. That is to say, there is an in-built pause between the sending of a message, and the sending of a reply. The messages are always complete, and there is no possibility of interruptions.

Mailing lists

These are based on the use of email. Instead of messages being sent between individuals they are sent to a central computer or 'server' for the particular list. From there they can be immediately copied and sent out to all the members of the mailing list. Mailing lists are usually free, and may be 'moderated', which means that a person reads the messages and decides whether it is appropriate to send them on to members of the list.

There are thousands of mailing lists covering a wide range of subjects. The degree of activity varies, but the more active ones can post many messages each day. They become similar to ongoing discussions.

Conferences

These are modifications of the mailing list procedures but use the same technology. Typically a 'conference' is announced and an expert is asked to post a 'keynote paper' on the mailing list. This will then be the subject of responses from members of the conference for a few days. Then a second expert contributes and/or responds, followed again by comment from members of the list. After all the subject areas have been explored one person summarizes the conference and issues the summary to all list members.

Usenet news groups

Up until this point we have been looking at systems where both the sender and reader are identified and where messages are automatically sent to the recipient or reader (or in the case of mailing lists only to those who have joined the list).

The usenet news groups operate by storing messages sent to the group rather like on a bulletin board. Anyone can then 'join' the group and read all the recent messages. They can also post messages themselves. There is no indication of who is reading the messages, anymore than the reader of a newspaper is individually identified. There are many thousands of these groups, which are indexed in a hierarchical way so that subject areas are broken down into more specialized sections.

Bulletin boards

These are similar to the usenet groups, but usually restricted to in-house networks or specialized groups.

Internet relay chat (IRC)

This is a system that provides a way of communicating in real time (ie synchronous communication) with people anywhere in the world. There are a number of networks of IRC servers. Each network may have over 10,000 channels, each devoted to a different topic. The 'conversations' are text based, but with a number of conventions which allow a small amount of expression of feelings etc., these include jargon abbreviations such as ttfn – ta ta for now, imho – in my humble opinion, j/k – just kidding, and so on. These act to make the conversations more 'real'. The conversations may be public or private. The users are known by nicknames, not their real names.

MUDs and MOOs

These rather strange sounding systems (and their derivatives such as MUSE, MUSH, TinyMUD) originated from the fantasy role-playing game 'Dungeons and Dragons'. In this game each player takes on the role of a character in the story: a warrior, elf, troll, sorcerer, etc. They are assumed to inhabit a maze of 'dungeons', which is a hypothetical world planned by the 'Dungeon Master' or game director. The Dungeon Master devises the rules which govern activity (and especially movement between dungeons) in this imaginary world, and as players decide to move around, they encounter beasts and obstacles. Only the Dungeon Master knows the full details of the fantasy world and its rules, although the players have some information. Players can develop their characteristics by acquiring attributes such as strength or speed together with objects such as keys, potions or weapons.

MUDs and MOOs were developed as computer based systems which mirrored the original idea. MUDs were Multiple User Dungeons but quickly became known by the more respectable sounding title of Multiple User Dimension or Multiple User Dialogue. The computer interacts with the role-players in accordance with the rules laid down by GOD (the General Organizing Director). The dungeons now become 'rooms' which the participant may visit and 'meet' with other participants. Thus the outcome of decisions depends partly on who else is playing.

MOOs are a development of MUDs, which are Object Oriented. That is to say they have a core purpose of exploring a particular subject. Thus one may have 'BioMOO' which is a virtual meeting place for biologists and the like. They mark the transition from entertainment games to educational games, and thence to educational conferencing facilities.

These systems are therefore similar to the IRCs, but with an added layer of a virtual world where there may be 'rooms' and participants may move from one room to another according to their interests. This has led to a number of 'Virtual Universities' where the different rooms represent meeting places to discuss and get information about specific subjects. There have been a few attempts to introduce graphics into the MOOs and MUDs, but on the whole they are text based.

World Wide Web (WWW)

The World Wide Web consists of several millions of 'pages' of information, which are stored on thousands of computers worldwide. Each WWW 'page' belongs to an individual or organization and may consist of one or more screen pages of text, pictures, sound loops, video or film clips. It may also house an index to a hierarchy of other WWW pages within the main or 'home' page. Every WWW page has a unique address, usually beginning http://. This address gets extended into the layers of sub-directories. Thus the BBC home page is:

http://www.bbc.co.uk. The BBC Education home page is: http://www.bbc.co.uk/education, health education is: http://www.bbc.co.uk/education/health, and so on.

It is the custom on WWW pages to include 'links' which are the addresses of other useful home pages. By clicking on these links with the mouse you can go directly to the other suggested pages which themselves will have links and so on ad infinitum.

There are now some very powerful systems, which enable the reader of a WWW page to interact with the material on the page and add text or other items to the page that is being viewed. This enables the user to fill in forms or send messages in response to prompts. There are also systems such as 'Virtual Places' (http://www.vplaces.com/Chatnow/index.html) which enable 'chat' to be overlaid on the background of a Web page. In this system the participant is represented by an 'avatar', a small picture or icon which appears on the screen together with a speech bubble when appropriate containing the text message.

A powerful tool in this system is that of the 'tour leader': one of the participants may invite others to move their avatars on to a tour icon such as a picture of a bus or plane and then to take the group to other pages where they can continue their discussions against a different background page, which may of course contain relevant information.

The power of the World Wide Web is in the combination of its graphic and sound capabilities, together with the ability for the user to move from one page in one part of the world to another page in another part of the world within seconds. This is combined with an infinite capacity for storage since the actual storage of information is distributed to an every increasing number of sites.

Potential uses of CMC and the Internet in role-play

Advantages

By using a little imagination one can see that there are great opportunities for using these tools to develop completely new types of role-play. One can get away from the usual restrictions of place and time. The participants may be anywhere in the world, and can extend their interaction over long periods of time, although this may mean asynchronous communication rather than real-time interaction. The participants may, if they wish, remain anonymous, and this enables them to play the part of any character irrespective of age, gender, status, or nationality. It is low cost and uninhibiting. Moreover, it is easy to keep records of the interaction for analysis afterwards.

By using some of the more advanced systems it is possible for a tutor to move the participants from one virtual environment to another. In addition, the computer can provide a data source which can be used as background information at any time, whether it is in the form of a database, a spreadsheet, or a WWW page.

Problems

Although the enthusiast will no doubt be stimulated to try out these systems, the technophobe will be more difficult to persuade. Unless they can see a clear advantage, it is likely that they will stick to face-to-face (f2f) role-play.

In their present form, the computer and network systems can be slow. In addition, if role-play extends over time-zones it is more likely to be asynchronous. No-one likes to get up at 2 am to take part in an international role-play, however exciting. There is also the problem of recruiting participants over wide areas, and of funding the activity, although as mentioned above, it is extremely cheap compared to normal experiential training exercises.

The actual process of CMC is different in that discussions take longer; the fact that contributions are written down means that they are more considered and more permanent than f2f contributions. This may inhibit participants and stifle spontaneity. In f2f groups the flow is fairly evenly paced. In CMC the flow may be a dribble or a flood. In CMC groups the tutor has little knowledge of inactive members and his or her interventions may be received by participants at different times; they cannot therefore be so finely tuned. In particular, there is no body language to modify first impressions.

There are also ethical issues, which centre on the relative lack of control which tutors have when dealing with a group of students at a distance since they cannot observe the emotional situation as easily as in face-to-face exercises.

A framework in Cyberspace

These then are the tools at our disposal. What ways can we find to use them? Clearly the stand-alone computer may be used to hold information. We may, for example, hold all the details of the characters in our role-play as a spreadsheet or database in the form of, say, a list of staff or inhabitants of an area. Details may be held of rules, and laws, or of financial matters. It is possible for the computer to hold details of role-play transactions or decisions.

With the networked computer it is possible to develop a text-based role-play between participants who are at a distance. This may take the form of email messages, or a real-time discussion via a chat channel. It will not be very long before it will be possible for these discussions to be on a sound channel, thus dispensing with text based communication.

When one adds the capability of the World Wide Web, and its graphical formats that enable one to view pictures and video, then it is possible to introduce documents, pictures, and all sorts of visual material to back up the role-play itself. The participants are able to refer to these documents and images whenever they want, and to share a lot of this information with each other during discussion. Moreover, the tutor may be able to change the environment from one location to another.

Looking into the future; examples of possible cyberspace role-plays

The field is at present characterized by a lot of talk but few relevant examples. Everyone is agreed that there is considerable potential; no-one seems to have actually developed a role-play using this potential to the full. Let us make an imaginative leap, however, and consider possible scenarios for two such role-plays.

Scenario One – Appointing a member of staff

The requirement is to train participants in interviewing and selection techniques, and also to make them aware of the other elements involved in recruitment and selection of staff, in particular the employment of disabled people and members of ethnic minorities.

The scenario is in fairly large organization, which has its own Human Resources Department (HRD), within which there is a personnel manager (PM), with a staff of three. Also within the HRD there is a training section (TS), which has a staff of four trainers.

The particular task in hand is to appoint a new trainer to replace one of the trainers who is leaving. There is a feeling that this new trainer should have a special responsibility for disadvantaged workers in the firm. There are four applicants shortlisted for the job.

Documentation and preparation

Details of applicants, with photographs of them and details of their current job are held on Web pages, which can be accessed by relevant participants. The applicants can amend these pages if they wish before the role-play begins. There are also details of the job description and conditions of employment held on the Web pages and available to all.

Details of conditions of employment, current salary, etc for individuals are held on Web pages but are only accessible to the individuals concerned.

There are also role-descriptions for all characters which are only accessible to the characters concerned. These include pictures of the person at work and pictures of their workplace together with pictures of them at home or taking part in their hobbies. This is all available only to specific people. These characters may be any or all of the staff of HRD and TS.

There will also be references for the candidates. These may be put together by the tutor, or written by other participants who can enter the role-play as previous employers. They may be contacted by the PM or others and 'interviewed' to get their views of the candidates. Thus this may be part of an on-going linked set of role-plays which extend organically in all directions. In the case we are considering, one of the candidates may be a school teacher or college lecturer, and the referees are the head of the school or college, and one of the candidate's current colleagues. Other candidates can be 'found' from role-plays which are based in social services or industry.

The tutor may decide to place the whole role-play in a virtual environment. Thus in this case the layout of the HRD offices and interview rooms may be described and used as part of the role-play to give it greater verisimilitude. In some cases this layout may be critical if two people need to meet without the knowledge of a third party, or if there are constraints of time or place on when the role-players are 'allowed' to meet.

Process

Each participant's computer will present to them the sequence of events from their point of view. This data may be downloaded from a central site. Thus it may say:

'You are one of the HRD administrators and have been asked to take part in the selection of a new trainer. Read your role description and amend it if you want. The amendments must be agreed by emailing the manager of HRD and asking for approval. You must then read the job applications and decide what questions you want to ask. When you have done this, let the PM know by emailing the dates and times that you can manage for interviewing the candidates.'

'You are PM. Read your role description and amend it if you want. The amendments must be agreed by emailing the manager of HRD and asking for approval. You need to arrange interviews for the four candidates. This can be done via email initially to the staff involved and then to the candidates. You will also need to involve the legal officer (LO) who will attend the interview and advise on employment law.'

'You are the legal officer (LO). It is your job to advise all participants on employment law. The following Web sites are applicable: note that for this particular set of interviews it will be necessary to know the law about the employment of disabled or disadvantaged people.'

'You have resigned as a trainer and your successor is being appointed. Some of your colleagues may contact you informally or you may meet them in one of the offices.'

There may also be details of the way in which role-players can move about the virtual world and who they may or may not meet. This opens up the possibility of the tutor playing the parts of an unlimited number of other people whom the participants may encounter as they seek to contact the other participants. These unplanned encounters may throw up additional information or constraints on the participants. If these encounters take place against the background of a Web page, with its graphical and multi-media possibilities, then the participant can be given a better picture of the virtual environment in which they are working. Pictures of the workplace and their colleagues can pinpoint the type of situation they are in.

Action

When a date and time has been set, the interviewers 'meet' via a chat-channel type of Internet system in order to discuss how the interviews are going to be conducted. This discussion can be in real time if the participants come from within the same or adjacent time-zones. If the role-play is being extended to participants across several time-zones the discussion may have to be partly asynchronous, with time lags between question and answer.

When the interviews have been organized, the candidates are asked to join the chat channel and the interviews take place. It will be possible for any number of people to 'listen in' on these interviews provided they have permission. Also it will be possible to keep an accurate record of them. During the interviews, participants can refer to information sources via Web pages which are either publically accessible, or only available to them. These Web pages will be a mixture of those that have been specially produced for the role-play, and those that are available in reality on the Web.

In parallel with this, the individual computers will be running presentation software that can remind participants of what areas they should be considering, and the sequence of actions they need to take. Some of the participants will be involved full time. Others, who may in real life be senior managers, may be getting on with their real job and only occasionally asked to enter into the on-going role-play.

Debriefing

At the end of the interview role-play, the tutor can open out the discussion to whoever is interested. As a result of the discussion it will be possible to re-run the role-play with a new set of participants, or to amend it to try certain elements with the same people. Moreover all the material will be available for any other tutor to use with their students.

Another possible outcome, which has been hinted at above, is that the 'characters' in the role-play may go on to participate in further role-plays which explore wider aspects of the firm, organization, or society.

Scenario Two – International marketing

This hypothetical scenario is designed to demonstrate the use of the Internet for a truly global role-play, which can involve players from different countries and different continents. The aim is to involve players in multilingual and multicultural environments in order to strengthen their linguistic abilities and provide a foundation for dealing across borders. Although it is written as a business training scenario, it could equally be used by schools for integrated and/or language studies.

The scenario is the marketing department of a multinational firm that wants to introduce a new product, say a new type of sweet, into a number of countries. It is assumed that the tutor can invite players from different countries to participate. This may involve the use of different languages.

Documentation and preparation

The documentation for the players will be similar to that prepared for the first scenario above. There will be role-descriptions for individual players together with data on manufacturing costs, packaging costs, advertising and direct mail costings, market research costs, etc. These will be held on computers and different data will be made accessible to different people according to their role and status.

In this case it may be that the roles have little 'character portraits' built in, although the hidden agendas of some players may be revealed to them only.

Their joint objectives are to plan a marketing and publicity campaign for this new product.

Action

This scenario depends very much on the ability to move players from one Web page to another. On the Web pages there will be pictures of the product and possible packaging. If the players decide they will pay for market research, then they will also have tables and graphs of consumer preferences in the different countries.

The role-players will have a series of meetings to decide on strategy and tactics. In between these meetings, in 'real time' they will have to think about the decisions and their implications. They may put up their own designs or suggestions on Web pages, and the meetings can then visit those sites and look at them while the discussion is taking place.

The role of the tutor is to control the timing and sequence of meetings, to move the players around the Web sites, and to keep a record of the discussions.

Debriefing

The debriefing can follow a similar pattern to that used in the first scenario. The role-players and observers can be given a transcript of the discussions and invited to comment on how they might have been handled more effectively. However, the experience of communicating across national boundaries, perhaps for the first time, will probably be sufficiently educational in itself, and require little debriefing.

Conclusion

In the course of this book we have looked at a wide range of role-plays and the techniques to deal with them. The choice is sufficiently diverse to provide tutors and teachers with a varied palette from which they can choose. By selecting well and planning work carefully they will find their role-play sessions are effective and enjoyable.

We have looked at the future. There is great potential in the use of computers and the Internet. No doubt those with the motivation, right environment and technical skills will experiment with this powerful medium. But there will always remain the basic need to expand the use of role-play as a means of helping people to develop life-skills. We can expect to see it used, for example, in teaching about assertiveness, race awareness, dealing with violence and disaster management. The ability to communicate is high on the list of transferable skills needed urgently by industry and the public service. And if it is possible to influence the traditional world of higher education – and here money can work wonders – it is possible that we shall see an increased use of these techniques in universities and colleges.

As the use of role-play spreads it is essential that the training of tutors in its use should be encouraged. It is a powerful tool and I hope that this book has given you the fundamental background to use role-play both wisely and with real enthusiasm. Enjoy using it, and your students will find learning an exciting and memorable experience.

References

Aston, D E (1985) *Management Games for Building, Vol. 1 Case Studies and Role Playing*, Chartered Institute of Building, Ascot

Blatner, H A (1973) *Acting-in: Practical Applications of Psychodramatic Methods*, Springer Publishing Company, Inc, New York

Bond, T (1986) *Games for Social and Life Skills*, Hutchinson, London

Boocock, S S and Schild, E O (Eds) (1968) *Simulation Games in Learning*, Sage Publications Inc, Beverly Hills/London

Brandes, D and Phillips, H (1979) *Gamesters' Handbook*, Hutchinson, London

Chesler, M and Fox, R (1966) *Role-Playing Methods in the Classroom*, Science Research Associates, Inc, Chicago

Cohen, L and Manion, L (1980) *Research Methods in Education*, Croom Helm, London

Collier, K (1998) 'Once more with feeling – identification, representation and the affective aspects of role play in experience-based education', in J Rolfe, D Saunders and T Powell (Eds) *The International Simulation and Gaming Research Yearbook Vol. 6. Simulation and Games for Emergency and Crisis Management*, Kogan Page, London.

Cooper, C L (1972) *Group Training for Individual and Organisational Development*, S Karger, Basel/London

Davison, A and Gordon, P (1978) *Simulations and Games in Action*, Woburn Press, London

Glandon, N D (1978) 'The hidden curriculum in simulations: some implications of our applications', in R McAleese (Ed) *Perspectives on Academic Gaming & Simulation 3*, Kogan Page, London

Haney, C, Banks, C and Zimbardo, P (1973) 'Interpersonal dynamics in a simulated prison', *International Journal of Criminology and Penology*, 1, 69-97

Jones, K (1980) *Simulations: A Handbook for Teachers*, Kogan Page, London

Ladousse, G P (1987) *Role-Play*, Oxford University Press, Oxford

Maier, N R F, Solem, A R, Maier, A A (1975) *The Role-play Technique: A Handbook for Management and Leadership Practice*, University Associates Inc, La Jolla, California/Mansfield, Notts

Milroy, E (1982) *Role Play: A Practical Guide*, Aberdeen University Press, Aberdeen

Moreno, J L (1953) *Who Shall Survive? Foundations of Sociometry, Group Psychotherapy, and Sociodrama*, Beacon House, New York

Pfeiffer, J W and Jones, J E (1974) *A Handbook of Structured Experiences for Human Relations Training* (several volumes), University Associates, La Jolla, California/Mansfield, Notts

Rackham, N and Morgan, T (1977) *Behaviour Analysis in Training*, McGraw-Hill, New York

Shaftel, F R and Shaftel, G (I 976) *Role-playing for Social Values: Decision-making in the Social Studies*, Prentice-Hall, New Jersey

Shaw, M E, Corsini, R J, Blake, R, Mouton, J S (1980*) Role-playing: A Practical Manual for Group Facilitators*, University Associates, La Jolla, California/Mansfield, Notts

Towers, J M (1969) *Role-Playing for Supervisors*, Pergamon Press Ltd, Oxford

Wohlking, W and Gill, P J (1980*) Role-playing: The Instructional Design Library*, Vol 32, Educational Technology Publications, Englewood Cliffs, New Jersey

Journals

There are no journals specifically devoted to role-play but the journals covering simulation and gaming usually have articles that deal with it.

A newsletter is published by SAGSET – the Society for Interactive Learning, Peter Walsh, 11 Lloyd Street, Ryton, Tyne and Wear, NE40 4DJ.

An International Yearbook on Simulation and Gaming is published by Kogan Page Ltd., 120 Pentonville Road, London N1 9JN.

An international journal which is US-based is *Simulation and Games*. It carries articles that cover the whole of the simulation/gaming field, not just those related to education and training. It is published by Sage Publications Inc, 275 South Beverly Drive, Beverly Hills, California 90212, USA. It is available in the UK from Sage Publications Ltd, 28 Banner Street, London EC1V 8QE.

Another source of information is the International Simulation and Gaming Association – ISAGA. Jan H G Klabbers, Oostervelden 59, 6681 WR Bemmel, Netherlands.

Index